Ethnologia Europaea

Journal of European Ethnology

Volume 47:2
2017

MUSEUM TUSCULANUM PRESS

Copyright © 2017	Ethnologia Europaea, Copenhagen
Printed	in Sweden by Exakta, Malmö 2017
Cover and layout	Pernille Sys Hansen, Damp Design
Cover photo	Photo manipulation by the artist Zacharie Gaudrillot-Roy (Façades 2–11)

ISBN 978 87 635 4611 9
ISSN 0425 4597

Ethnologia Europaea is an official journal of Société Internationale d'Ethnologie et de Folklore (SIEF).

sief

Museum Tusculanum Press
Dantes Plads 1
DK-1556 Copenhagen V
Denmark
www.mtp.dk

CONTENTS

Antti Lindfors
Performance of Moral Accountability and the Ethics of Satire in Stand-up Comedy   5

Britta Lundgren
Health Politics, Solidarity and Social Justice. An Ethnography of Enunciatory Communities during and after the H1N1 Pandemic in Sweden   22

Niels Jul Nielsen and Janus Jul Olsen
Flexicurity without Security. An Inquiry into the Danish Flexicurity Model in a Neoliberal Era   40

Anastasiya Astapova
When the President Comes. Potemkinist Order as an Alternative to Democracy in Belarus   57

Jernej Mlekuž
"We Asked for Workers. We Got Bureks Instead". Meanings and Material Significance of the Burek in Slovenia   72

PERFORMANCE OF MORAL ACCOUNTABILITY AND THE ETHICS OF SATIRE IN STAND-UP COMEDY

Antti Lindfors, University of Turku

This paper explores one particular approach to satire in stand-up comedy, a popular cultural genre of oral performance, which is at the intersection of emotion and ethics. It is suggested that morally charged emotional language is particularly situated in stand-up due to the interactionally engaging features of this genre. The argument consists in framing satire as a practice and performance of moral accountability. The analysis explores how the invocation and potential dramatization of moral accountability and (intentional) agency dialectically enhance the emotional and moral efficacy of satire, and why certain habitual practices constitute fruitful targets for satire. Several cases are presented to examine how satire gives rise to dialectic of moral accountability and emotion through the use of specific stylistic and textual devices.

Keywords: satire, accountability, morality, emotion, stand-up comedy, performance

One of the stereotypical, reified images evoked by the popular cultural genre of stand-up comedy certainly includes a person raging in front of others, as a spectacle of anger – an image encapsulated distinctively in the comic personas of 1990s American performers like Andrew "Dice" Clay and Denis Leary (see Peterson 1997; Ahmed 2004). The attributes of "brutal honesty", "shamelessness", and "unruliness", frequently invoked by both practitioners, followers, and advertisers of stand-up alike, underpin this impression of (emotional) liberty and fearlessness as some of the genre's most reiterated metapragmatic emblems (e.g. Louis C.K. 2007; May 2015). While potentially construed as commercial aestheticizations of emotion from just one perspective (e.g. Jameson 1991; Meštrović 1997), these attributes also hint at the nature of stand-up comedy as an intimate and interactionally engaging form of performance clearly laden with heightened expectations of responsibility and competence for performers and audience members alike. Apart from apparent character comedians, one could read the action of *standing* in stand-up comedy as implying a heightened moral standard (cf. Limon 2000). Prototypically speaking, stand-up comics stand behind their personas and words while often demanding similar accountability and interactional investment from their audiences.

In the following text, I explore the understandings and practices of emotion and satire in the performance genre of stand-up comedy. Emotion provides an analytically compelling objective in the context of this genre, insofar as stand-up performances are mimetically structured around an emulation of spontaneous conversation while also regularly invoking, inviting, and playing with strong affective responses from the audience. Although one should obviously hesitate to label stand-up as an art form dedicated to deception, it is fair to say that it is based on certain "contrived misperception" (Taussig 2006: 123). In this regard, the very *leitmotif* of stand-up comedy could be construed as one of the double binds famously articulated by Gregory Bateson ([1972]2000): "Be spontaneous!" This illusion of immanence, which in stand-up is coupled with a metacultural embrace of newness (Urban 2001; see also Wilce 2009b: 31, 34) that encourages improvisation and authenticity, intersects in interesting ways with the ongoing research into emotions as interactional, performative, and embodied phenomena (for immanence in the theatrical arts since the 1970s, Lehmann 2006: 18, 145–152, 96–97; Fischer-Lichte 2008: 18, 22–23).

With an eye on what he labels the "reportability" of narratives (also known as tellability), William Labov (1997, 1972) generalized three thematic areas worthy of recounting across different cultures: "The universal principles of interest […] dictate that certain events will almost always carry a high degree of reportability: those dealing with death, sex and moral indignation." It needs to be mentioned, though, that such formulations that have to do with absolute standards of reportability have been heavily criticized using more context-sensitive perspectives (e.g. Norrick 2005; Goldstein & Shuman 2012; also Savolainen 2017). In any case, by spinning their yarn around any of these subjects, comics may well increase the odds that listeners will be captivated. While it is not uncommon for stand-ups to discuss death at a very personal level – for instance in the Finnish stand-up scene I have been following, Anitta Ahonen is known for frequently addressing heavy topics such as cancer and death, and Joni Koivuniemi has openly dealt with his mother's passing as part of his set – and sex figures as a major thematic hub of stand-up even to the point of compromising its tellability (i.e. becoming hopelessly clichéd), it is safe to say that moral indignation is not far behind.

It is in the latter focus that I am primarily interested in the current effort.

Preliminary Remarks

Moral indignation can be conveyed in comic contexts by using the stylistic and communicative device of satire; more often than not it also serves as a comic motive. Satirists are affectively invested in their cause, for they claim to "speak 'from the heart,' from a sense of acute, unmediated anger" (Rosen 2012: 2), which can be historically traced back to satire's roots in magical curses and taunts (Elliott 1970). Of the varieties of humorously inclined expression, satire can be seen as an exceptionally "passionate" and engaged mode of discourse, in contrast with the (perceived) more distanced nature of many other types of humor and irony (cf. Oring 2003: 78; Chatman 2001: 30; Bergson 1935).

I propose that we should approach satire as an everyday communicative device (rather than, for example, just a literary genre) that can be heuristically understood as a form of ironic discourse that engages with ethics in very specific ways. Downplaying the conventional viewpoint of satire as only negative social critique and emphasizing the multimodal affordances and interactional aims of stand-up comedy as oral performance, I focus on how satire traces and invokes a sense of moral accountability for the positions of both the producer and the target of satire. The presumption is that this can be fruitfully done by concentrating on instances of multimodal satirical texts that manifest elaborate and/or extended fabrication, thus bringing forth this invocation of accountability. In this regard, a particularly interesting viewpoint of this discussion is the notion of intentionality, as far as the latter constitutes a prominent aspect of the broader idea of agency.

I first address the issues of emotion, accountability, and emotional expression in stand-up comedy by elaborating on what can be described as emotional management or the instrumental use of emotion signs in ritualized performances. Taking cue from the character of stand-up comedy as an elusive performance genre that simultaneously builds on interactional investment and responsibility, I argue for a semiotically informed approach, by focusing on the pragmatic aspects of emotional expression in social interaction. This approach will be illustrated by looking at a sequence of stand-up from a recent commercial release by the popular South African comic Trevor Noah, which also can serve as a bridge to the following section on satire and ethics. Here I develop an outline of satire as a practice and performance of moral accountability that places its emphasis on the cultural and social ramifications of satire instead of its more formal or technical definition.

In the final section I apply this conceptual framework to the topic and develop some of its further implications by using various examples, most notably my field recordings of the Canadian-Finnish comic Jamie MacDonald. This material consists of performances by MacDonald, which were recorded in Helsinki during late 2016 in the context of documenting material for my dissertation. I have been drawn toward societally and politically oriented or what has elsewhere been called "charged" (Krefting 2014) comedy, and paid particular attention to the intersections between stand-up comedy and satire from the perspective of their concomitant communicative forms and contexts. The various examples presented in this paper, while perhaps seemingly disparate or sparing in quantity, represent a discretionary sample of ongoing work that I have chosen with an eye for their relevance to problematize the interactional dynamics of satirical stand-up comedy.

Rather than adhering to the conventions of a classic ethnographic research article, I prefer to characterize the following discussion as an argument for thinking through the practices of satire and comedy using fresh theoretical perspectives and as an outline of a novel definition of satire. Consequently, the theoretical and methodological basis for this approach is also delineated as a combination of various sources. Even though my disciplinary home remains in folkloristics, and that background continues to prime me toward variations in cultural expression, performance, and group dynamics, I have now drawn freely from related academic fields, such as (linguistic) anthropology, semiotics, cultural theory, and humor studies. It is my contention that socially central and culturally inexhaustible phenomena, such as comedy and satire, not only deserve but also require interdisciplinary perspectives without which their analysis would remain inexorably tenuous.

Ration Your Passion: The Emotional Expression in Stand-Up

Insofar as stand-up comics may be considered ritual specialists, the presentation and management of appropriate emotions (with respect to genre, occasion, narrative storyline, etc.) is a core element of stand-up performances. Emotional expression is particularly highlighted in stand-up, as the bodily co-present interactional set-up of the genre generally demands engagement, investment, and involvement of its audiences in performance – most obviously by their voluntarily joining in on the collective laughter (for more on the intimacy and distance in stand-up, see Brodie 2014). Such intimacy and social cohesion, however ephemeral or temporary both may turn out to be, is effectively produced by performers through their use of emotional language. Comparably, modalities and genres of discourse like personal confessions, opinionated stance-taking, and gossip, that both imply and invoke heightened forms of accountability, provide comics with potent means for interactional engagement (relatedly in terms of confession and gossip, see also Robbins & Rumsey 2008: 409).

More often than not, emotional language use and moral judgments are also closely intertwined. For instance, disgust is an especially efficient emotion that is deployed for (corporeally) authenticating moral judgments, or rather *moralization* in the sense that the practice of labeling others' behavior as disgusting or shameful is functional in constructing hierarchical distinctions between perceived normality and abnormality (Paasonen 2011: 88–89; Warner 2000: 4).

Earlier, I adopted the notion of "management" so as to integrate various textual, poetic, narrative, gestural, spatiotemporal, and interactional aspects of stand-up performances from the perspective of the performer (Lindfors forthcoming a; forthcoming b), and I suggest that emotional expression can be approached in the same way. Management pushes us to focus on how means are organized toward a fixed set of goals and in this case on how conventions of emotional language are instrumentally used by stand-up comics in interaction (cf. Scheer 2012: 209; Reddy 2001: 122).[1] Given certain qualifications, the notion of "emotional management" can additionally override the still dominant Western conception according to which emotions are thought and spoken of as preceding their expression via verbal or non-verbal modalities (Lutz & White 1986; Wilce 2009a).

A case could be made against conventional views that locate emotion safely in subjective inwardness by simply recalling that emotions are communicated through public expressions that fall under a speaker's metapragmatic awareness and can be thus explicitly reflected on. This aspect is all the more obvious in the specifically "framed" environments of performances that both contain and open up these (potentially negative) expressions to inspection and aesthetic valuation (Bendix 2015; Beeman 2007: 286). Secondly, emotional expressions are understood as having an effect on those states to which they seemingly are only just referring (Reddy 2001: 103–104, including the citations). As William M. Reddy points out, public, personal expressions of emotion ("emotives" in Reddy's terminology, although not to be confused with Jakobson's [1960] classic use of the term) are performative in the sense that, as expressions, they are organizing experience. James M. Wilce (2009a: 10–12) similarly recalls that human action frequently makes use of indexical signs that precede their referents: emotion signs do not merely reflect some prior causes of which they are the effects; they may themselves have entailments as when we provoke emotional states in ourselves.

These ideas shake the foundations of the received wisdom that views performances of emotion through the lenses of "sincerity" or "authenticity" – two notions that also organize stand-up comedy to a high degree (Colleary 2015: 41–66; Reddy 2001: 101; Fenigsen & Wilce 2012; Keane 2002). In terms of stand-up comics, this means that whether or not comics regularly feel the (extreme) emotions they present, they certainly do use the verbal and non-verbal conventions of the emotion signs available to create the possibilities for intersubjective states with their audiences (Wilce 2009b: 47; Scheer 2012: 214). Authenticity or "accuracy" of an emotional expression is thus not necessarily ascertained by any reference to supposed inner states or intentions, but rather is a function of its coherence with other co(n)-textual utterances, gestures, and acts (Reddy 2001: 100).[2]

To refine our take on emotional expression as well as gradually orient ourselves toward the specifics of satirical discourse, I suggest we acknowledge emotion signs as operating on all three Peircean levels, namely, the iconic, indexical, and symbolic. Not only are emotion signs often read as indexical, causal or "natural" emissions associated with psychological or physiological states, the iconic similarities inferred from their discursive and sensuous qualities can vary according to context, and their conventionalized symbolic meanings have been shown to be as historically and ideologically volatile as those of any other communicative signs (Wilce 2009a). These qualities are brilliantly invoked, objectified, and playfully explored in the latest stand-up special by Trevor Noah (*Lost in Translation*, 2015), a South African comic whose fame skyrocketed in 2015 when he replaced Jon Stewart as the host of *The Daily Show*, a long-time spoof news show that satirizes current events. I thus want to briefly introduce a sequence from this performance before moving on to satire as a morally and affectively charged communicative device.

In a sequence that follows seemingly organically from his entrance onto the stage (starting at approximately 30 seconds into the commercial recording), Noah explores the indexical, performative, and (mock-)etiological aspects as well as the ideological mediation of what appears to be a seemingly natural, raw emotional interjection. When well-known comics enter the stage, an audience is regularly expected to holler, applaud, whistle, and express their excitement in various ways. At first thanking, greeting, and welcoming the audience, Noah eventually picks up on one of these hollers, juxtaposes this style of communication with propositional language use, and lifts a specific emotional interjection up for inspection:

> This is us, Washington D.C! [cheers and applause] Are you guys feeling good? Yeah! Whoo-hoo, whoo-hoo to you… and that as well, ma'am, that as well. I love the sounds people make. It's so much fun, yeah. We're just – we're just throwing language out of the window, I like that. I feel like we're devolving as human beings now. No, 'cause that was the thing that separated us from the apes, wasn't it? The fact that we chose speech. Yeah. The monkeys used to run around and screech. [screeching while mimicking the gestures of apes] And we, we're like, "No." [points to the side] – "English." But now we've started to go back to that, started to embrace our roots. People get excited: "Are you happy?" – "I'm real happy." – "How happy?" – "Whoo-hoo-hoo-hoo!" "Whoo-hoo!" [writhes and twists himself]. (Noah 2015)

In short, Noah objectifies the embodied emotion sign of *whoo-hoo*, renders it explicitly available to reflective awareness. This emotion sign seems to be marked by its aural, but also its embodied, gestural, and other sensuous qualities, such as the facial expression and the bodily writhing that Noah exemplifies when emitting the sound. His embodied performance of the interjection illustrates what Webb Keane (2003: 414–415) describes as the *bundling* of sensuous qualities in iconic signs, as well as the bringing into relief of some of these qualities that is typically a function of simultaneous indexicality. That is, while we might intuitively associate the aural qualities of *whoo-hoo* as indexical of its social significance (excitement, "happiness"), these qualities are inescapably bundled with various other sensuous qualities of the interjection that "can become contingent but real factors in its social life". The fact that Noah is able to take the interjection as an object of explicit attention and perform it without actually "engaging" with it, without meaningfully using it, in turn provides the yet-to-become-significant proof that the purportedly self-evident qualities of such "spontaneous" signs are also outcomes of naturalization. In other words, in everyday use, the intense sound *whoo-hoo* is naturalized as an icon of an intensified "inner state" as well as an index of an emotion that Noah labels "happiness".

Next, Noah contrasts the seemingly self-evident, natural roots of the interjection with what is generally regarded as anything but self-evident – the domain of ideologies.

> And you know what's crazy is that we all know what that sound means. We don't agree on anything in this world – race, religion, politics – but that sound, that "whoo-hoo", has united us all. You can make that sound anywhere, and people accept it. As long as there's alcohol present, you can make that sound whoo-hoo! But there has to be alcohol. (Noah 2015)

By extrapolating from this apparently agreed-upon nature of emotional interjections, Noah suggests how this specific interjection has "united us all". There are some contextual qualifications, however. Working from "alcohol" as an experiential boost, Noah goes on to explain how you cannot emit the sound in the office, nor in church after common prayer. But in any case, he recapitulates that it is commonly taken for granted that everyone knows what *whoo-hoo* means: "It means happiness, yeah. It means the happiness of the people."

A fracture to this logic emerges when Noah notes that he personally would not have "picked" this particular sound as the sound of happiness: "No one asked me to vote on it. I didn't get to choose." From him, we hear, *whoo-hoo* might be more apt as the sound of sadness, a notion that is elaborated on through dramatization of a funerary rite. The prototypical indexical value of "happiness", then, seems not to adhere to the interjection or the sound *by itself*, but rather is unveiled as an outcome of conventional agreement and typification. Not only does iconicity entail indexicality, as Noah seems to remind us, but indexes and icons both entail (potentially contested) symbolic and ideological mediation for them to become intelligible and functional socially as tokens of a type (Keane 2003).

Having finished exploring what is understood as the primarily indexical aspects of the said interjection, the mood of the performance changes slightly as Noah moves on to what I call a racially oriented mock-etiological account of the origins of this emotion-sign:

> Such a fun sound. The sound of happiness. *The sound* [raises voice] of white happiness, in particular. Yeah… I've tracked it. I've searched for the source of "whoo-hoo" and I found it originated with white people. White – white woman, in particular. Yeah, that's where it comes from. That is the sound, of a white woman's turn-up. That is the sound of her getting into the game. (Noah 2015)

Noah traces the etiological origins, or "the source" of the interjection – somewhat playfully no doubt, although outwardly, he still appears perfectly serious – to white people, white women in particular, who can thus be held accountable for its social value and meaning. He relates this information as his own, the result of his investigations, calling forth a sense of engagement, as the audience can receive this piece of knowledge first-hand. Moreover, he discloses the interjection not only as a joyful sign of white group-identification, but also as a social and sexual signal by which white women "instinctively" draw the attention of white men, who reciprocate by mimicking the call. In other words, this interjection is described as performatively functioning as a "mating call". It is suggested that the sound has mimetically, "as a virus", expanded onto the society and other groups and from the "natural" and "instinctive" use of white women to a "learned" use by everyone else. And so, the very different experience of black people is ultimately occasioned against this framing background:

> Black people whoo-hoo, but it's not the natural sound black people make for fun, you know? Black people can whoo-hoo. Black people often do whoo-hoo. But it's not instinctively a black sound of happiness. And I think it's because black people aren't comfortable with the "whoo-hoo".

Deep down inside, there's a certain moment in whoo-hoo when every black person stops enjoying it. There's just – there's just a moment, when – and maybe this is just my personal experience but I fear it sounds eerily similar to a police siren. [laughter arises] There's just a moment when it stops being fun. [laughter and cheers continues] There's just that split second, where it's like "whoo-hoo", "whoo", "whoo", "whoo", "whoop-whoop", "whoop", "whoop", "boop" [the interjection transforming into the sound of a siren]. (Noah 2015)

The long preface for developing this seemingly off-the-cuff topic – an individual interjection – is thus revealed as a stylized elaboration of satire on racial relations in the U.S. In short, to be anxiously reminded of the police by an everyday interjection has to be read as also being hyper-oriented toward the police. Noah develops the theme further by narratively dramatizing his own experience and anxiety as a black subject in close contact with the police force, which then leads into a long discussion of institutional racism in recent U.S. social history. By first invoking the incident of Trayvon Martin followed by the cases of Mike Brown, Eric Garner, and Walter Scott – innocent black men killed at the hands of the police during recent years – he ultimately unfolds his concerns explicitly, without a hint of irony: "Cause every day I turn on the TV, it seems like another black person has been shot."

To take a step back, the satirical footing of the speaker as well as the target of the satire are keyed by the appropriately incongruous (Oring 2003) association of a police siren with an emotion sign that has been framed by Noah as an emblem of predominantly "white" happiness. Recalling once again the fact that indexical signs necessitate ideological mediation, the satire here seems to be instrumentally manipulating these mediational processes. In other words, it flouts our ordinary ideological assumptions according to which interjections ("oops", "phew", "whoo-hoo"), seemingly spontaneous, embodied emotion signs, would be immune to confabulation and historical and political manipulation. After all, interjections have been traditionally located at the very periphery of language. They are something that Herder thought of as the human equivalents of animal sounds and in modern linguistics are still regarded as being "nearest of all language sounds to instinctive utterance" (Sapir 1921: 6–7; Kockelman 2003). The motivation for a "natural", indexical sign that we would not normally regard as politically or ethically charged, is thus playfully denaturalized.

Characteristically for satirical discourse, the suggested interpretation is playful fabrication (cf. Simpson 2003: 167; Haugerud 2013); folklorists here recognize an etiological legend, a narrative that purports to explain the origin of something (see Oring 2008). Yet what interests me is precisely what is being accomplished by this elaborate fabrication or legendry. In short, its function seems to relate at least in part to *the priming, contextualizing, and gestation of a particular moral accountability upon which the eventual satirical punch of the routine is emotionally and causally dependent*. While presenting itself as a neutral description, Noah's satire seems to indirectly suggest that something is not as it should be, that a certain someone ("the whites") could and should be held accountable for this state of affairs – even more so as the satire has been uttered by one who is a member of the group of people being wronged.

Satire and Ethics: Toward a Heuristic Model

Satire is not something only professional comics are able to master; it is a basic, arguably, even mundane, communicative device and discursive practice (Simpson 2003). It is generally described as a "venomous", "biting", or "stinging" critique of hypocrisies, ideologies, or "vices" present in society (for attributes such as "venom", see Elliott 1970; for satire as targeting "social vices", Draitser 1994: xxi). Further still, satire tends to be intuitively aligned with "progressive" social interests – providing us with the first hint of the culture-specific linguistic ideologies related to this discursive practice that associate specific people with certain linguistic forms – even though claims for satirical purposes are naturally heard from other social and political fractions as well. While perhaps handy as a provisional elaboration, such an evaluative and possibly normative starting point is hardly useful in any rigorous analytical context. Whose "vices" and "hypocrisies" are we talking about, after all? What does this "venom" or "bite" entail? And how does satire differ from mere irony that is also deemed to be a form of negative critique (Rahtu 2006; Hutcheon 1994; also Shoaps 2009)?

As a metapragmatic label for a discourse practice or device, satire is identified as having a minimum of two positions, one of which is construed as the target of the satire, while the other is its producer, that is, the one responsible for the satirical text (both positions naturally indexing alignments with presupposed systems of sociocultural value, see Du Bois 2007). As is also known, whether or not some communicative event is satirical or whether the event can be construed as such, and what are the ramifications of such an interpretation, frequently becomes the very bones of contention in the explicit social and ethical debate. It is even possible to argue that satire has no stable ontological status, as Paul Simpson has pointed out. The status of "satire" rather emerges in interaction: it is *conferred* upon the text or performance as a consequence of the inferential work done by its recipients (Simpson 2003: 153). This means that both the targets of satire and the intentions of the satirist are conferred and mapped onto the performance, which thus increases the satire's social contentiousness to the point where explicit metapragmatic reports by the satirist ("what I said was meant as satire") can be invalidated by recipients.

The prominently value-laden nature of satire as a metapragmatic label is also manifested in that cultural texts and performances representing worldviews and moral codes foreign to one's own – let us say satire carrying racist implications if we are determinedly anti-racist – are not easily granted the status of satire but perhaps preferably regarded as coarse or insulting ridicule (symptomatically, see, e.g., Webber 2013: 57). Didier Fassin's (2012) remark concerning the interpretation and even the mere description of moral facts as always being at risk of normative positioning is thus clearly pertinent here, and as I hope to convincingly argue, has to be understood as also including the labeling of a discursive artifact as satirical. To summarize, the problem of satire as an *analytical* concept is that it might insidiously recruit the objects of analysis and the analyst herself to a partial and normative framework that may not actually be at play for the agents and groups under study (to paraphrase Nakassis 2012: 717 on brands). This aspect is something that will be kept in mind as I here gradually outline my own, heuristic approach to this device and discursive practice.

When satire is approached as a communicative device and discursive practice used in everyday interaction and performance – rather than as a literary genre, as strong tradition would have it – it is typically articulated with irony, if not also humor. As a point of departure, it is fairly noncontroversial to suggest that a necessary feature of satire is an ironic, negative comment with respect to some chosen target. For instance, Simpson (2003: 99) argues that the impetus of satire is a certain *disapprobation* by the satirist of some aspect of the satirized target, and then extrapolates from this view by suggesting that "all categories of satirical target can ultimately be expanded upwards to encompass the discursive practices of elite groups, dominant institutions or powerful individuals" (2003: 148). And insofar as practices are designated as systematically forming the objects of which they speak (e.g. Foucault 1972), satire thus emerges as inherently performative, or rather, as counter-performative.

Simpson further claims that satire is built on what he dissects as a "double irony", and thus, I would suggest that we simply look at satire as a form or subcategory of irony (see Simpson 2003: 90 and onwards; also Rahtu 2006). The difference between irony as a broader, more neutral term and satire as its singular subcategory, I argue, is that satire specifically engages with ethics and morals in both the positions of target and producer. While earlier research has certainly taken note of this aspect of satire, as an area of sustained focus, it seems to nevertheless have remained underdeveloped and often implicit. Still, remarks such as Northrop Frye's famous definition of satire as "militant irony", noting how satire requires "at least an implicit moral standard" (1957: 224, 233–234), and W.H. Auden's claim that a suitable satirical target was someone who transgresses "the moral law" ([1952]1963: 383–384), do indeed point the way. Revealingly, Auden added that anyone who lacked the "normal faculty of conscience" (the wicked and the lunatic are Auden's type examples) is unsuitable for this position. In other words, the target of satire has to be both capable of moral responsibility and committed to that responsibility.

Taking my cue from Auden, I propose that satire generally functions by way of tracing, invoking, and attributing moral accountability, and thus by implication, an agency. Whereas irony is very much possible in accidental and unintentional situations and settings, our linguistic ideologies dictate that satire depends on a target that falls within the purviews of moral accountability (on "sarcasm", cf. Haiman 1998). Sometimes this accountability is distributed across a broader social field (via various rhetorical framing devices for example), as when we satirize certain institutional practices or even large-scale processes like "modernization" or the general *Zeitgeist* (see Enfield & Kockelman 2017). On occasion, it can be concentrated into a single agent, be it a named person (e.g. politician) or a corporation whose liability is being raised (cf. Hill & Zepeda 1992: 197). In any case, it is the moral integrity of the target that is brought into question as somehow reprehensible. Ralph M. Rosen (2012: 29) refers to this "driving" aspect of satire as its "didacticism" and puts it thusly: "The guiding premise of all satire […] is that something is not 'as it should be,' and it takes a satirist to set the world straight."

Attributions of accountability and agency are endemic to social life, just as intention-seeking is a basic human propensity. Indeed, the two are intertwined aspects of social behavior in the sense that ethical reasoning typically involves ascriptions of intention and motivation (Keane 2016; Laidlaw 2010; Williams 1993). However, depending on cultural sensibilities and (ontological) assumptions, accountability and responsibility can also be assigned to nonhuman agents and entities: spirits, gods, supernatural forces, etc. Attributing moral responsibility to corporations, on the other hand, makes it reasonable to satirize their practices. Illuminatingly, this can be done by metaphorizing such entities as discrete agents with voices, intentions, even emotions. The point worth raising here is that in the latter case of corporate responsibility, the notion and implications of agency cannot be reduced to intentionality or "conscious planning", but must rather be understood as encompassing the more general theme of wielding power or having an effect on social reality (Duranti 2004: 453). Intentionality presupposes agency, not the other way around.

Finally, it seems to me curiously symptomatic that while self-parody and especially self-irony are well-established notions and popular activities, also among stand-up comics, the label of "self-satire" does not seem to be part of our common vocabulary. While part of the problem is presumably related to the popular or intuitive conception of satire as a form of outwardly directed social critique, I propose that this aspect is also – if not more intimately – connected to satire's invocation of moral accountability. Self-irony is often directed at features of oneself that are perhaps more lightly discounted (appearance, body image, personality traits, viewpoints and opinions, etc.), but satirizing oneself, I believe, would imply a more thoroughgoing and (ambivalently) serious critique of one's own ethical constitution or moral integrity as a social being.

That being said, it is perfectly possible for the satirist to have taken part in (institutional) practices that are the targets of her satire. Universal methods of calibrating the narrating-I with the narrated-I in first-person narratives (see e.g. Herman 2013; cf. Double [2005]2014: 393–408; Seizer 1997), for instance, enable speakers to denounce their antecedent actions or personas morally, that is, in a manner that could be labeled self-satirical. In fact, an ethical incongruity of the kind has been recognized as defining "postmodern cynicism", a condition in which we routinely act in accordance with prevailing ideological norms (of market liberalism, consumerism, etc.) while simultaneously (mis)recognizing these norms as false, detrimental, or oppressive. In such sociopolitical and cultural predicament in which also humor may "cease to struggle" (Sloterdijk 1987: 305; also Boyer & Yurchak 2010; Yurchak 1997), the notion of self-satire might as well become regarded as contradictory or even conceited.

With these preliminaries in mind, satire can be heuristically outlined as *a form of irony that is characterized by its ethically accountable and emotionally charged target, which is perceived (and insinuated) by the satirist as being morally reprehensible*. Not so much a definition as an invitation, this model is hardly detailed technically, as it does not say much about the mechanism for how satire works. However, following the suggestion of the humor scholar Seppo Knuuttila (1992), I chose to begin with the aims and purposes of the study and tried to steer the attention toward the social and cultural ramifications of satirical discourse as a practice and performance of moral accountability instead of its formal definition or technical details (cf. also Hutcheon 1994). Next, I develop the further implications of this framework in the context of stand-up performance by looking at an example drawn from fieldwork.

Satire as Performance of Moral Accountability

By attributing and assigning accountability and agency, does satire give rise to both of these qualities? Judith Butler (1997: 45–47) would probably side with this performative viewpoint, insofar as she notes by drawing on Nietzsche that the subject often appears only "as a consequence of a demand for accountability." She refers to the fact that we tend to isolate the causes of events and doings in intentional agents, simultaneously producing and figuring these agents as singular subjects. By purposefully raising the question of moral accountability, satire can similarly foreground or recast chains of events or casual behavioral patterns as intentional, meaningful actions of agentive beings – a direction that Trevor Noah's routine also pointed toward. One way of achieving this seems to work by transforming "natural" signs into seemingly "non-natural" ones, so as to simultaneously invoke notions of accountability (for such transformations, see Grice [1961]1989); however, the methods of satire are not reducible to this element. If satire may have a tendency to treat surrounding events as meaningful signs, perhaps expanding the field of social agency in the process (cf. Laidlaw 2010: 157), this would indicate that the purpose of satire is to trace ethically accountable targets. Moreover, if we accept the premise that satire is indeed "play with a bite to it" (to borrow from Moira Marsh [2015: 66] expanding on Gregory Bateson), the sort of stylized dramatization of (intentional) agency described above can be intimately linked with just the emotional and moral "bite" in question (cf. Oring 2016: 104).

I will now turn to an instance in which an individual agent (although representing a group, the neo-Nazis) is discursively mobilized in the service of satire to see how satire gives rise to the above-mentioned dialectic of moral accountability and emotion by the use of various stylistic and textual devices. The following transliteration constitutes a sequence from a performance by Jamie MacDonald, a Canadian-born stand-up comic who has lived in Finland for fourteen years (the video material is in possession of the author). MacDonald is a transgender man who has dealt with aspects of his gender reassignment process as part of his stand-up – the reason I bring this point up relates to the fact that the following routine also turns on the trope of gender transition.

The performance partly transcribed below was recorded on December 11, 2016, in Helsinki at a club called Feminist Comedy Night (hosted by MacDonald himself), and should be contextualized by understanding the prominent rise of both populist and far-right political movements as well as outright neo-Nazis in Finland (following on the heels of their international counterparts, of course). In fact, the bit was first performed on September of the same year at another stand-up club in Helsinki, Kekkosklubi, a week after a man named Jimi Karttunen had died in Finland while opposing a demonstration of the neo-Nazi organization Suomen Vastarintaliike ("Finnish Resistance Movement"), as a result of an assault by a member of that same organization. In the stated performance on September, which I also saw, MacDonald first took issue with media for dealing with the death incident ignorantly, for asking "What had Jimi done to provoke these Nazis?", and secondly, for juxtaposing neo-Nazis with immigrants. According to MacDonald's proposed syllogism, juxtaposing and "tolerating" both neo-Nazis and immigrants is a false or skewed balancing act, because while a portion of immigrants are Muslims, and a portion of Muslims are angry Jihadists, it does not follow directly that all immigrants will be Jihadists – while contrarily all (neo-)Nazis are indeed Nazis.

Similarly, in the performance recorded in December, MacDonald lays the groundwork for his routine by reminiscing on related protest against fascism and neo-Nazism and by elaborating on the renegotiation of Leftist identity in an unprecedented societal and political situation (in Finland) where one has to deal with self-proclaimed Nazis. In particular, he recounts how he had recently had to rework his idea of tolerance "now that there are actual, [...] literal Nazis around." Again pointing out a rhetorically skewed and ungrounded demand for reciprocal balance, he quotes the Nazis as demanding the liberal Left "to be tolerant of white supremacists" in the same measure that the Left demands equal rights for minorities, immigrants, women, etc. Rather than elaborating on the familiar problem of "tolerating intolerance", MacDonald promptly invokes the notion of causal necessity: "Were you born a Nazi? I don't think so."

Importantly, in both performances, MacDonald's main targets seem to have been constituted by public discursive practices that share logical and moral fallacies: 1) the discursive practices of the media, and 2) the discursive practices of neo-Nazis, both of which are represented and criticized as skewed and unsound. However, a sociopolitical debate or a critique such as this one does not in itself constitute satire: first of all, nothing particularly ironic has yet been uttered. That is to say, the properly satiric (as well as more artistic and elaborate in terms of performance) sequence of this particular routine is yet to come, namely, consisting of a counterfactual imagining of turning to Nazism as a transition along the same lines as a gender reassignment operation:

1a   that's kind of the tautology there
1b   and it's not like you kind of…
1c   people think you kind of like wake up in the morning like […]
2a   "I think I'm gonna…
2b   I – I identify now as a Nazi
2c   I – I wanna like, you know
2d   I gotta, you know, change my political orientation"
3a   and people'll be like:
3b   "When did you first know that you were a Nazi?"
     [turning over to his right, questioning an imaginary interlocutor]
4a   "I was very young, I was a child, I heard *Finlandia* [L]
     [repositioning himself spatially to his right while turning slightly over to his left to answer an imaginary interlocutor]
4b   and… one time I shaved my head and… it looked really right [L]
4c   I just went into… went into the mirror and I…
4d   you know, I put on my bomber jacket from my cousin and I did this salute in the mirror
     [raises left arm in a Nazi salute]
4e   and it just looked like me
     [open left palm touching chest]
4f   so, I want to 'Nazition'"

MacDonald juxtaposes some of the stereotypical phases related to newfound gender identification with discovering and identifying with Nazism as a political and social orientation (this implicit juxtaposition was made even more salient in the earlier performance on September when MacDonald set the imaginary conversation as having happened in a "Nazi clinic"). While this is not the place to discuss mutual interrelations and theoretical discussions regarding gender and (biologically perceived) sex, this sequence is conditioned by the premise that whereas gender identification is regarded as causally predetermined by natural constraints, holding or supporting ideological systems, such as Nazism or fascism, is in contrast an intentional choice which one can – and should – rationally oppose. The satirical superimposition of the two domains is functional in highlighting the moral accountability that we associate with voluntary (and generally harmful) identifications such as (extreme) political affiliations in contradistinction with gender identifications that are seen as predetermined, necessary, personal, and most definitely non-harmful. In this regard, the foundational opposition between causal determination and free will emerges as one of the most powerful tropes that satirists seem to lean on (cf. with Trevor Noah's invocation of an opposition between the natural vs. "learned" use of the *whoohoo* interjection).

I would like to remind the reader here that what is critically targeted by the comic is presumably still reprehensible discursive practices held and publicly reiterated by certain groups, not necessarily individuals, even though an individual agent is explicitly mobilized here for satirical purposes. We could say that certain (fabricated) consequences or "logical" outcomes of these discursive practices are illustrated by the comic through the use of a brief scene. Bearing this focus in mind, consider how and why the experience and the mindset of the imaginary Nazi-transitioner is then foregrounded by various stylistic and textual devices. Most importantly, the counterfactual scene is mostly enacted rather than recounted, which intensifies the visual and perceptual experience of the scene by narrowing the (temporal) distance between the narrated event and the ongoing performance event. Embodied enactment allows the comic to gesturally portray the actions from the perspective of the target agent, which iconically enhances the vividness of the sequence. The sequence is further layered with direct quotations that expressively portray and give us access to the mindset of this agent. The epiphanic realization of the would-be-Nazi is verbalized as a string of repetitive clauses that highlight and dramatize his or her intentions by placing the emphasis on desires and moods (2a–2d). Similarly, the phases of physical readjustment to a new "political orientation" (4a–4d) are described in a way reminiscent of what Keane (2016: 86–87) labels as "overdescription of the action". Briefly put, the method of "overdescription" constitutes a purposeful violation of the Gricean maxim of quantity ("be as informative as is required") in the sense that by willfully drawing attention to the verbose or otherwise overly descriptive quality of utterance, such as listing individual action sequences discretely, speakers are understood as specifically intending to enhance the emotional and moral efficacy of their accusations.

The formal technique utilized by the comic here is one of parody, parodying the stereotypical phases (and phrases, e.g. 3b) related to adapting to a newfound gender identification, as depicted through aesthetic, corporeal, and sartorial practices. The sequence culminates in a pun ("Nazism" and "transition" equals "Nazition") that succinctly captures the creative juxtaposition and cognitive blending of these two frames (see also Simpson 2003). Finally, the sequence is framed by the comic – and I will come back to some of the implications of this framing in a minute – as a general practice with farther-reaching ramifications rather than as an idiosyncratic fancy ("people think you kind of like wake up in the morning like").

What should one make of such an extended dramatization and enactment of intentional agency? First of all, in the context of an interactionally engaging genre of oral performance such as stand-up comedy, vivid gestural enactments and indirect forms of expression may be seen as increasing communicative efficiency by drawing audiences in to participate in meaning-making (see Besnier 1992: 163). (In addition, such an artistically elaborate sequence seems to receive the biggest laughs from the audience, not the least of which is due to curious details such as the portrayal of Jean Sibelius' *Finlandia* hymn as triggering the political conversion process in childhood.) However, I believe that the emphasis on intentional agency bears implications regarding to satire, and even more so if we follow through on the theoretical outline of satire as engaging with moral accountability.

In general, "causal accounting, as the figuring (out) of agency, tends to focus on those causes that are particularly relevant to the agents who are doing the accounting" (Kockelman 2017: 16; also Keane 2016: 80; Carroll 2001; Drew 1998). What is meant here is that we purposefully foreground those aspects of agency that we deem relevant to whatever context or situation we might be inhabiting and whatever interactional or social ends we might be pursuing – for instance, criticizing or satirizing (or alternatively praising) certain targets. It is fair to assume that similar fine-tuning with respect to the definition of the situation takes place when people attribute responsibility and accountability to others and their actions, and I suggest that the technique of foregrounding (intentional) agency in satire must be understood in terms of this self-serving premise. Each of the textual devices and small stylistic choices highlighted above, such as the "overdescription" and the mimetic, gestural reenactment of the scene, are seen as participating in this emphasis on intentional agency, so it becomes more reasonable to simultaneously (if only implicitly) invalidate and ridicule the actions being depicted. More precisely, it becomes reasonable to ridicule the false logic of the discursive practices from which these counterfactual actions could potentially follow.

I would also like to draw attention to the fact that satire often targets what appears to be habitual action, unpacking it as *intentional and yet lacking self-awareness*. Habitual actions, in this case, have to be understood as encompassing both the discursive and the verbal as well as embodied and non-verbal practices. To clarify, it is possible for an actor to do something both intentionally and without awareness at the same time – in fact, this mode can be argued as constituting the very notion of the habitual. By necessity, a lion's share of our routine, everyday actions and doings are performed below the reasonable level of awareness, and yet it would be a clear mistake to deem these actions as unintentional. For example, when swimming (given that I am a competent swimmer) I am very much intentionally performing the embodied, patterned movements that constitute that particular action sequence. But this fact does not translate to the idea that I would consciously *be aware of* my embodied actions at all times. In contrast, the fact that I *do not* have to consciously focus and fixate on these movements means they have been ingrained in my embodied habitus practically – indeed, gestures form a major domain of the habitual (Young 2011). These movements and actions have been sedimented into habitual practices, to "an intentionality not necessarily based on propositional thought" (Scheer 2012: 203; Duranti 2015: 20–21; also Throop 2010: 40–41). In addition, practices are fruitful targets for satire, I would argue, because un-self-aware practices are interpreted as unconscious responses that are driven in large measure by unregulated emotions.

In this regard, it is indeed illuminating to look at the intersections between satire and the structural setting and dynamics of practical jokes as analyzed by the folklorist Moira Marsh (2015). In practical jokes that are specifically organized to cultivate a moral comment (not all are), the performative frame that is unilaterally imposed on the unassuming target importantly also builds on and plays with the (attributed) intentional mindset of the target. Practical jokes will frame the (reprehensible) actions of the target as his or her own intentional doing, consequently fixing the responsibility of the action on the target's own shoulders and thus satisfying "our thirst for poetic justice on small-time wrongdoers" (Marsh 2015: 60). In particular, Marsh explains how the logic of practical jokes does dictate that "targets are not acting but being themselves, unwittingly putting themselves on display" (Marsh 2015: 63). The description of "unwitting" action here has to be understood as an ideal expectation by the joker, as for the practical joke to work ideally, the target must be acting "unwittingly", or at least the quality of "unwitting" action has to be attributed to him in terms of interpretative acts. Needless to say, this quality as identified by Marsh, which I have here described as "un-self-aware and yet intentional", also constitutes the general domain of habitual practices.

Consider lastly here the following satirical quip by the British stand-up comic, Stewart Lee, known as a politically liberal or Leftist performer (as well as a columnist for *The Guardian*). He starts an episode of his *Comedy Vehicle* (Season Four, Episode Two) dealing with Islamophobia by calmly asserting: "Like most reasonable people, I hate all Muslims, except the ones I've met, who seem fine." By following the line of reasoning developed in the current article, we can say that through parodic imitation, Lee presents Islamophobia as a habitual practice of unfounded and self-conflicted hatred. This practice is depicted as feeding on unreflective prejudice and crumbling upon the slightest hint of personal experience with the object of hatred. Stylistically, the un-self-aware intentionality of the parodied mindset is, once again, emphasized by a simplified – almost syllogistic – clause syntax that enhances the satirical effect by giving rise to the appearance of habitual self-evidence. By implying that the Islamophobe follows what appears to be highly scripted behavior, the full agency of this target is both questioned and ridiculed, insofar as "any habitual behavior pursued unreflectively makes us foolish and vulnerable" (Marsh 2015: 68; cf. Bergson 1935). To also take Lee's trademark deadpan delivery into account, it is intriguing to note that his paralinguistically and gesturally unmarked, deadpan form of expression produces and underscores this habitual behavior through an iconic resemblance. That is, the unreflective and unmarked casualness on the level of embodied expression, which becomes salient in the context of crude Islamophobia, metapragmatically diagrams itself as an icon of an unreflective and habitual social practice.

Concluding Remarks

It is the guiding premise of this article that satire can be regarded as a form of ironic discourse that engages with ethics and morals in very specific ways. In particular, I have explored the idea that the target of satire has to be one to which moral accountability (and by implication, the potential for agency) can and should be attributed. Further, I have looked at how this dynamic is harnessed and dialectically dramatized to enhance satire's emotional and moral efficacy in comic performances. I would like to emphasize here that satire does not necessitate elaborate dramatization of *intentional* agency. There are plenty of satirical cartoons and jests, for instance, that depict their targets as one-dimensional stereotypes without sparing much explicit thought on the issue of intent. That is, satire often depicts (fabricated) outcomes or consequences and seems to concern itself explicitly with *who* has done or continues to do *what*, rather than *why* something occurred (see Duranti 2015). However, intentions and purposes can be regarded as something that satire addresses or points toward even in the absence of any explicit dramatization.

As importantly, I have considered it valuable to broaden our perspectives on satire by problematizing it in various communicative environments, including embodied oral performances. Insofar as communicative media, channels, and contexts have their particular purposes and (visual, verbal, aural) affordances for meaningful expression, these outlets also bring variegating aspects of common stylistic devices, such as satire, into greater light. In particular, interactionally engaging genres of performance, such as stand-up comedy, seem to favor gestural and embodied (re)enactments that enable its performers to vividly portray intentional or habitual agency by affording a visual supplement to verbal narration (also Lindfors forthcoming b).

I have also drawn attention to the fact that habitual practices seem to provide satire with suitable targets in that 1) practices are by definition recurrent, conventionalized, and socially influential, not coincidental or idiosyncratic, and 2) as intentional actions of agentive beings, they articulate intimately with notions of accountability. What is more, satirists seem to draw pleasure from targeting their ridicule specifically on the unaware, sedimented nature of many practices, thereby simultaneously questioning their moral integrity. Veena Das (2012: 139) points out that because of the "strong emphasis on intentionality and agency in our contemplation of ethics, habitual actions are often reduced to 'mere behavior'". The Western domain of the moral foregrounds conscious agency and decision-making, which is inversely seen with Euro-American satire insofar as satirical texts tend to dramatize these aspects of behavior. However, by articulating habitual actions with intentionality, I have looked at how satire can interrogate or counter such tendencies by showing us how habitual practices are also suffused with moral aspects and choices. Satirical attacks on (morally reprehensible) habitual practices can be thus construed vis-à-vis the classic Bergsonian viewpoint according to which laughter corrects behavior that has become too mechanical, and can thus bring out "the human" – the moral – in us (Bergson 1935). In doing so, satire provides its users with an efficient tool to provoke moral stances from their audiences, which as a tendency can be said to constitute important (ethno-)methodological and epistemological aspects of this multipurpose communicative device.

It is an inherent aspect of any study of satire – one that should be answered by analyzing cases in their ethnographic contexts and taking into account the broader repercussions of satirical texts – to question whether this communicative device actually serves any higher good by unveiling "truths" or triggering democratic debate, instead of merely circulating negative stereotypes of its targets and in the worst case supporting the cynical point of view according to which "things never change". The focus on the (attributed and dramatized) moral accountability that is presented here can be understood as partaking in the same problem, but from a complementary angle, especially when we should regard such attributions and dramatizations as potentially rendering the targets of satire more multi-dimensionally and morally approachable.

Cultural and social analysts need to pay attention to satire and stand-up comedy insofar as these cultural forms regularly engage with and comment on such fundamental aspects of social behavior as accountability, agency, and concomitant perceptions of intentionality – and are able to do so with considerable traction. In this respect, I would give the final word here to Paul Kockelman (2017: 22), who has recently mused as follows: "In some sense, the most consequential forms of agency reside in who or what determines what counts as agency, and thus who or what should be held accountable as an agent."

Notes

1 The *locus classicus* inevitably invoked by "emotional management" is of course the work of Arlie R. Hochschild (1979, 1983). While I want to acknowledge her

pioneering research on emotion work and emotional labor, my own semiotically informed approach differs from hers in consciously abstaining from assuming any "true" emotions within a person that would become shaped for the purposes of emotional labor or management.

2 To broaden the perspective, one should also take into account the linguistic ideologies that dictate specific valuations of interrelated linguistic forms and contexts: cultural and social contexts that privilege concerns with personal sincerity, an example being the Protestant West, often distrust ritualized (emotional) expression because of its perceived "emptiness" deriving from conventionality (Robbins 2001, esp. pp. 598–599).

References

Ahmed, Sara 2004: *Cultural Politics of Emotion*. New York: Routledge.

Auden, W.H. (1952)1963: Notes on the Comic. In: *Dyer's Hand and Other Essays*. London: Faber and Faber, pp. 371–385.

Bateson, Gregory (1972)2000: *Steps to an Ecology of Mind*. Chicago & London: The University of Chicago Press.

Beeman, William O. 2007: The Performance Hypothesis: Practicing Emotions in Protected Frames. In: Helena Wulff (ed.), *The Emotions: A Cultural Reader*. New York: Bloomsbury Publishing, pp. 273–298.

Bendix, Regina F. 2015: Cultural Expression and Suppression of the Undesirable and Unbearable in Everyday Life: An Introduction. *Ethnologia Europaea: Journal of European Ethnology* 45:2, 5–13. (Special issue: *Rage, Anger and Other Don'ts.*)

Bergson, Henri 1935: *Laughter: An Essay on the Meaning of the Comic*. London: Macmillan.

Besnier, Niko 1992: Reported Speech and Affect on Nukulaelae Atoll. In: Jane H. Hill & Judith T. Irvine (eds.), *Responsibility and Evidence in Oral Discourse*. Cambridge: Cambridge University Press, pp. 161–181.

Boyer, Dominic & Alexei Yurchak 2010: American Stiob: Or, What Late Socialist Aesthetics of Parody Reveal about Contemporary Political Culture in the West. *Cultural Anthropology* 25:2, 179–221.

Brodie, Ian 2014: *A Vulgar Art: A New Approach to Stand-Up Comedy*. Jackson: University Press of Mississippi.

Butler, Judith 1997: *Excitable Speech: A Politics of the Performative*. New York: Routledge.

Carroll, Noël 2001: *Beyond Aesthetics: Philosophical Essays*. Cambridge: Cambridge University Press.

Chatman, Seymour 2001: Parody and Style. *Poetics Today* 22:1, 25–39.

C.K., Louis 2007: *Shameless*. HBO Special. Directed by Steven J. Santos.

Colleary, Susanne 2015: *Performance and Identity in Irish Stand-Up Comedy: The Comic 'I'*. Basingstoke: Palgrave Macmillan.

Das, Veena 2012: Ordinary Ethics. In: Didier Fassin (ed.), *A Companion to Moral Anthropology*. Malden, MA: Wiley-Blackwell, pp. 133–149.

Double, Oliver (2005)2014: *Getting the Joke: The Inner Dynamics of Stand-Up Comedy*. 2nd edition. Bloomsbury: Methuen.

Draitser, Emil A. 1994: *Techniques of Satire: A Case of Saltykov-Ščedrin*. Berlin: Mouton de Gruyter.

Drew, Paul 1998: Complaints about Transgressions and Misconduct. *Research on Language and Social Interaction* 31:3, 4, 295–325.

Du Bois, John W. 2007: The Stance Triangle. In: Robert Englebretson (ed.), *Stancetaking in Discourse: Subjectivity, Evaluation, Interaction*. Philadelphia: John Benjamins, pp. 139–182.

Duranti, Alessandro 2004: Agency in Language. In: Alessandro Duranti (ed.), *A Companion to Linguistic Anthropology*. Malden, MA: Blackwell, pp. 451–473.

Duranti, Alessandro 2015: *The Anthropology of Intentions: Language in a World of Others*. Cambridge: Cambridge University Press.

Elliott, Robert C. 1970: *The Power of Satire: Magic, Ritual, Art*. Princeton, NJ: Princeton University Press.

Enfield, N.J. & Paul Kockelman (eds.) 2017: *Distributed Agency. Foundation of Human Interaction*. Oxford: Oxford University Press.

Fassin, Didier 2012: Introduction: Toward a Critical Moral Anthropology. In: Didier Fassin (ed.), *A Companion to Moral Anthropology*. Malden, MA: Wiley-Blackwell, pp. 1–17.

Fenigsen, Janina & James M. Wilce 2012: Authenticities: A Semiotic Approach. *Semiotic Inquiry* 32:1, 2, 3, 181–200.

Fischer-Lichte, Erika 2008: *Transformative Power of Performance: A New Aesthetic*. Florence: Taylor & Francis.

Foucault, Michel 1972: *The Archeology of Knowledge*. New York: Harper and Row.

Frye, Northrop 1957: *Anatomy of Criticism: Four Essays*. Princeton: Princeton University Press.

Goldstein, Diana E. & Amy Shuman 2012: The Stigmatized Vernacular: When Reflexivity Meets Untellability. *Journal of Folklore Research* 49:2, 113–126.

Grice, Paul (1961)1989: The Causal Theory of Perception. In: *Studies in the Way of Words*. Cambridge, Mass.: Harvard University Press, pp. 224–247.

Haiman, John 1998: *Talk is Cheap: Sarcasm, Alienation, and the Evolution of Language*. New York: Oxford University Press.

Haugerud, Angelique 2013: *No Billionaire Left Behind: Satirical Activism in America*. Stanford: Stanford University Press.

Herman, David 2013: *Storytelling and the Sciences of the Mind*. Cambridge, Mass.: MIT Press.

Hill, Jane H. & Ofelia Zepeda 1992: Mrs. Patricio's Trouble: The Distribution of Responsibility in an Account of Personal Experience. In: Jane H. Hill & Judith T. Irvine (eds.), *Responsibility and Evidence in Oral Discourse*. Cambridge: Cambridge University Press, pp. 197–225.

Hochschild, Arlie R. 1979: Emotion Work, Feeling Rules, and Social Structure. *American Journal of Sociology* 85:3, 551–575.

Hochschild, Arlie R. 1983: *The Managed Heart: Commercialization of Human Feeling*. Berkeley: University of California Press.

Hutcheon, Linda 1994: *Irony's Edge: The Theory and Politics of Irony*. London: Routledge.

Jakobson, Roman 1960: Closing Statement: Linguistics and Poetics. In: Thomas A. Sebeok (ed.), *Style in Language*. Cambridge: MIT Press, pp. 350–377.

Jameson, Fredric 1991: *Postmodernism, or, The Cultural Logic of Late Capitalism*. Durham, NC: Duke University Press.

Keane, Webb 2002: Sincerity, "Modernity", and the Protestants. *Cultural Anthropology* 17:1, 65–92.

Keane, Webb 2003: Semiotics and the Social Analysis of Material Things. *Language & Communication* 23, 409–425.

Keane, Webb 2016: *Ethical Life: Its Natural and Social Histories*. Princeton & Oxford: Princeton University Press.

Knuuttila, Seppo 1992: *Kansanhuumorin mieli. Kaskut maailmankuvan aineksena*. Helsinki: Finnish Literature Society.

Kockelman, Paul 2003: The Meanings of Interjections in Q'eqchi' Maya. *Current Anthropology* 44:4, 467–490.

Kockelman, Paul 2017: Gnomic Agency. In: N.J. Enfield & Paul Kockelman (eds.), *Distributed Agency*. Foundation of Human Interaction. Oxford: Oxford University Press, pp. 15–23.

Krefting, Rebecca 2014: *All Joking Aside: American Humor and Its Discontents*. Baltimore: Johns Hopkins University Press.

Labov, William 1972: *Language in the Inner City: Studies in the Black English Vernacular*. Philadelphia: University of Pennsylvania Press.

Labov, William 1997: Some Further Steps in Narrative Analysis. *Journal of Narrative and Life History* 7:1–4, 395–415.

Laidlaw, James 2010: Agency and Responsibility: Perhaps you can have too much of a good thing? In: Michael Lambek (ed.), *Ordinary Ethics: Anthropology, Language and Action*. New York: Fordham University Press, pp. 143–164.

Lehmann, Hans-Thies 2006: *Postdramatic Theatre*. Abingdon: Routledge.

Limon, John 2000: *Stand-Up Comedy in Theory, or, Abjection in America*. Durham & London: Duke University Press.

Lindfors, Antti (forthcoming a): Twin Constellations: Parallelism and Stance in Stand-Up Comedy. *Oral Tradition* 31(2).

Lindfors, Antti (forthcoming b): Spatiotemporal Management of Stand-Up Performances: Narration and Gestures.

Cultural Analysis: An Interdisciplinary Forum on Folklore and Popular Culture.

Lutz, Catherine A. & Geoffrey M. White 1986: The Anthropology of Emotions. *Annual Review of Anthropology* 15, 405–436.

Marsh, Moira 2015: *Practically Joking*. Logan: Utah State University Press.

May, Ralphie 2015: *Unruly*. Available on Netflix.

Meštrović, Stjepan G. 1997: *Postemotional Society*. London: SAGE.

Nakassis, Constantine V. 2012: Counterfeiting What? Aesthetics of Brandedness and BRAND in Tamil Nadu, India. *Anthropological Quarterly* 85:3, 701–721.

Noah, Trevor 2015: *Lost in Translation*. Online streaming (http://trevornoah.com).

Norrick, Neal 2005: The Dark Side of Tellability. *Narrative Inquiry* 15:2, 323–343.

Oring, Elliott 2003: *Engaging Humor*. Urbana: University of Illinois Press.

Oring, Elliott 2008: Legendry and the Rhetoric of Truth. *Journal of American Folklore* 121:480, 127–166.

Oring, Elliott 2016: *Joking Asides: The Theory, Analysis, and Aesthetics of Humor*. Logan: Utah State University Press.

Paasonen, Susanna 2011: Kielletyn hedelmän haju. In: Siru Kainulainen & Viola Parente-Capková (eds.), *Häpeä vähän! Kriittisiä tutkimuksia häpeästä*. Turku: Utukirjat, pp. 84–103.

Peterson, Michael 1997: *Straight White Male: Performance Art Monologues*. Jackson: University Press of Mississippi.

Rahtu, Toini 2006: *Sekä että: Ironia koherenssina ja inkoherenssina*. Helsinki: Finnish Literature Society.

Reddy, William M. 2001: *The Navigation of Feeling: A Framework for a History of Emotions*. Cambridge: Cambridge University Press.

Robbins, Joel 2001: Ritual Communication and Linguistic Ideology: A Reading and Partial Reformulation of Rappaport's Theory of Ritual. *Current Anthropology* 42:5, 591–614.

Robbins, Joel & Alan Rumsey 2008: Introduction: Cultural and Linguistic Anthropology and the Opacity of Other Minds. *Anthropological Quarterly* 81:2, 407–420.

Rosen, Ralph M. 2012: Efficacy and Meaning in Ancient and Modern Political Satire: Aristophanes, Lenny Bruce, and Jon Stewart. *Social Research: An International Quarterly* 79:1, 1–32.

Sapir, Edward 1921: *Language*. New York: Harcourt, Brace.

Savolainen, Ulla 2017: Tellability, Frame, and Silence: Emergence of Internment Memory. *Narrative Inquiry* 27:1, 24–46.

Scheer, Monique 2012: Are Emotions a Kind of Practice (and what is that which makes them have a history)? A Bourdieuian Approach to Understanding Emotion. *History and Theory* 51:2, 193–220.

Seizer, Susan 1997: Jokes, Gender, and Discursive Distance

on the Tamil Popular Stage. *American Ethnologist* 24:1, 62–90.
Shoaps, Robin 2009: Moral Irony and Moral Personhood in Sakapultek Discourse and Culture. In: Alexandra Jaffe (ed.), *Stance: Sociolinguistic Perspectives*. Oxford: Oxford University Press.
Simpson, Paul 2003: *On the Discourse of Satire: Towards a Stylistic Model of Satirical Humor*. Amsterdam: John Benjamins.
Sloterdijk, Peter 1987: *Critique of Cynical Reason*. Minneapolis: University of Minnesota Press.
Taussig, Michael T. 2006: *Walter Benjamin's Grave*. Chicago: University of Chicago Press.
Throop, C. Jason 2010: In the Midst of Action. In: Keith M. Murphy & C. Jason Throop (eds.), *Toward an Anthropology of the Will*. Stanford, California: Stanford University Press, pp. 28–49.
Urban, Greg 2001: *Metaculture: How Culture Moves Through the World*. Minneapolis: University of Minnesota Press.
Warner, Michael 2000: *The Trouble with Normal: Sex, Politics, and the Ethics of Queer Life*. Cambridge: Harvard University Press.
Webber, Julie 2013: *The Cultural Set-Up of Comedy: Affective Politics in the United States Post 9/11*. London: Intellect Ltd.
Wilce, James M. 2009a: *Language and Emotion*. Cambridge: Cambridge University Press.
Wilce, James M. 2009b: *Crying Shame: Metaculture, Modernity, and the Exaggerated Death of Lament*. Maiden, MA: Wiley-Blackwell.
Williams, Bernard 1993: *Shame and Necessity*. Berkeley: University of California Press.
Young, Katherine 2011: Gestures, Intercorporeity, and the Fate of Phenomenology in Folklore. *Journal of American Folklore* 124:492, 55–87.
Yurchak, Alexei 1997: The Cynical Reason of Late Socialism: Power, Pretense, and the Anekdot. *Public Culture* 9, 161–188.

Antti Lindfors, M.A., is a Ph.D. candidate in the Department of Folkloristics at the University of Turku, Finland. His forthcoming dissertation deals with the popular cultural genre of stand-up comedy from the combined perspective of textuality, intimacy, and performance management. He works in the research department of the Finnish Literature Society in Helsinki.
(anmili@utu.fi)

HEALTH POLITICS, SOLIDARITY AND SOCIAL JUSTICE
An Ethnography of Enunciatory Communities during and after the H1N1 Pandemic in Sweden

Britta Lundgren, Umeå University

During the H1N1 influenza pandemic 2009–2010 in Sweden, a mass-vaccination intervention was enacted as a precautionary measure. Half a year later, medical authorities reported an increased incidence of the life-long neurological disease narcolepsy, later firmly established as a side effect of the pandemic vaccine. Using interview material together with archived protocols, this article presents an analysis of two communities, the National Pandemic Group and the Narcolepsy Association. The aim is to discuss their respective ways of arguing for solidarity, herd immunity, social justice and claim for culpability of the state. Both communities face dilemmas, doubts and double-bind situations, but also perform politics and ethics for the future in mobilizing notions of solidarity and responsibility in their different narratives.

Keywords: H1N1 pandemic, health politics, solidarity, vaccination, narcolepsy

Waiting for an influenza pandemic

In spring and summer of 2009, national and global news media overflowed with stories of a new influenza pandemic. As history has shown, influenza pandemics have had an impact on public health, economy, and societal functions, and since the Spanish flu of 1918–1919, public health authorities regard them as health threats. Furthermore, they are now matters of national and international security, for health, societies, and states. Most high- and middle-income countries prioritize pandemic preparedness, thus strengthening emergency infrastructure and stockpiling antiviral pharmaceuticals and vaccines (Lundgren & Holmberg 2017).

Despite this kind of advanced pandemic preparedness (cf. Lakoff 2008; Barker 2012; MacPhail 2010: Holmberg & Lundgren 2016), the 2009 pandemic brought new challenges to public health governance. It came with an unexpected virus (H1N1 instead of the anticipated H5N1), started from an unexpected place of origin (Mexico and California instead of Southeast Asia), and afflicted mainly young and middle-aged people. Medical risk groups were pregnant women, the morbidly obese, and the chronically ill. Besides the perceived threat to children and young adults, this pandemic was also different from earlier pandemics in other ways. A report from the European Centre for Disease Control states, "it was the first pandemic with instant communication, so that early impressions … could be shared ahead of proper scientific analysis." "Instant communication" implied among other things that the blogosphere and other communications tools needed to be acknowledged (Leung & Nicoll 2010). Charles Briggs and Daniel Hallin have from the perspectives of anthropology and media studies analysed how the news coverage and media logics were incorporated into the processes and practices of different actors during the pandemic in the United States (Briggs & Hallin 2016). As also could be said about Sweden, the pandemic involved "a kind of fusion of science, the state, and media, a largely harmonious collaboration between health officials and mainstream journalists" (Briggs & Hallin 2016: 134; cf. Gherzetti & Odén 2010).

Influenza gives rise to epidemics on a smaller or greater scale each year. An influenza pandemic on the other hand, is caused by a virus strain with a genetic composition and antigenic setup not previously encountered by the global population. Neustadt and Fineberg have referred to influenza as a "slippery disease" because the virus is complex and constantly mutating, making vaccines less effective than for many other diseases. In addition, influenza symptoms are often confused with those caused by other viruses, making it hard to estimate the effects of the virus from year to year (Neustadt & Fineberg 1978).

The H1N1 pandemic (popularly known as swine flu) reached Sweden in the late summer and autumn of 2009. In accordance with the pre-pandemic preparedness, Swedish authorities effectively implemented a strategy for handling the pandemic, including a mass-vaccination intervention as soon as the vaccine Pandemrix would become available in October. At the time, I was working as a Dean of the Faculty of Arts at Umeå University in Sweden. As for most people then, my knowledge about the pandemic was influenced by information from Swedish politicians, health authorities and media debates, including reports from Mexico, California, and the southern hemisphere. During meetings with the Vice-Chancellor and the other Deans, we discussed what kind of responsibilities we should take as a university, for example, how we should facilitate the vaccination of our employees as soon as possible. Several questions occurred. Was it wise for a group of leaders (myself included) from the university to participate in a planned delegation trip to China, Taiwan, and Australia in September of that year? Moreover, on a personal level, would I be able to persuade my two sons, aged 17 and 21, to take the shot? My concerns were allayed – university employees were vaccinated at their workplaces, my two sons were also vaccinated (as was I), and the delegation trip was completed successfully. My recollections of encounters with the pandemic during the trip are about details such as fever monitoring at some airports, worried or accusatory glances if someone coughed too heavily on the airplane, and our frequent use of hand sanitizers. At that time, I was certainly not thinking of the pandemic as a future object for my own research.

The pandemic has been my research focus since 2013 with the overarching aim to investigate different cultural and social framings concerning the pandemic and the vaccination measures in Sweden.[1] The project has been intermixed with ongoing efforts to integrate ethnology and humanities into the medical field, and the concept of *medical humanities* into the fields of culture and history (Lundgren 2013, 2015a). My work has resulted in a recursive journey into what would unfold as epistemic labyrinths of the pandemic, oscillating between interviews as the main source, together with observations, media reports, and archived protocols from different authorities. It also meant making excursions into (for me as an ethnologist) unknown territories of knowledge, including infectious diseases, immunology, virology, vaccinology, and epidemiology. Some textbooks in the fields of infectious diseases and epidemiology encouraged the integrated cultural-epidemiological approach to "highlight the creative interdisciplinary ways by which researchers are confronting today's vexing and complex health challenge" (cf. Trostle 2005: 3). However, more common were the strictly bio-medically informed paradigms governing science, conferences, and funding agencies. The fields of medical anthropology, applied anthropology and science and technology studies became the academic in-between-landscapes where it was possible to combine the two (cf. Martin 1994; Farmer 1999; Nichter 2008; Singer 2015; Briggs & Hallin 2016).

As Laëtitia Atlani-Duault and Carl Kendall noted in 2009, the responses to the pandemic was overwhelmingly biological and epidemiological in scope. They proposed a research agenda for anthropologists to "play an important and underutilized role in planning and responding to influenza and other global emergencies" (Atlani-Duault & Kendall 2009: 207). Such a research agenda would explore more comprehensive, but perhaps uncomfortable truths, in focusing for example on politics, government, economy, religion and history (2009: 210). In my research project, I have tried to tackle the issue of the pandemic as a broad concept to investigate several subject areas and themes, at times distant from the usual pathways for Swedish ethnological research.

So far, the project has resulted in publications on pandemic preparedness (Lundgren & Holmberg 2015; Holmberg & Lundgren 2016), on lay people's perceptions of the immune system in relation to the common cold vs. influenza (Lundgren 2015d), and on attitudes towards vaccination (Lundgren 2015c). They have also focused on different aspects of narcolepsy as a side effect (Lundgren 2015b; Lundgren & Holmberg 2015), on issues as solidarity, trust and ethics (Lundgren 2016; Lundgren & Holmberg 2015), and on influenza pandemics and vaccination in history (Holmberg 2016; Lundgren & Holmberg 2017).

In this article, I will concentrate on two main actors in the Swedish narrative of the pandemic: the National Pandemic Group (NPG) and the Narcolepsy Association (NA). With inspiration from Kim Fortun (2001), I will call these actors *enunciatory communities*, both facing emerging doubts and dilemmas throughout the course of the pandemic and its aftermath. My aim is to discuss their respective ways of using concepts such as solidarity, herd immunity, social justice and claims of culpability of the state. The juxtaposing of these two communities enables a discussion about how public health politics, notions of collectivities, risk and uncertainty intervened into the process of pandemic response in Sweden.

The Swedish Pandemic Narrative

With the help from evaluations and other official documents, it is easy to construct a broad Swedish narrative about the swine flu. It contains different spatio-temporal ingredients such as the pre-pandemic planning and preparedness starting in 1993, and an advanced purchase agreement in 2007 with a vaccine producer (GlaxoSmithKline) in case there would be a need for a new vaccine. There is the reported outbreak in California and Mexico at the end of April 2009 and the WHO upgrading the epidemic into a pandemic on June 1. It also involves the (almost) consensual and effective decision-makings in the face of this upgrading, and a successful national mass-vaccination campaign with logistics in place and over 60% uptake. Sweden also has the advantage of possessing specialized facilities for treating the most severely ill – the ECMO-ward at the *Karolinska University Hospital* in Stockholm (ECMO = extracorporeal membrane oxygenation). The pandemic eventually turns out to be milder than expected with a very low case of fatality (MSB & Socialstyrelsen 2011).

The mass-vaccination intervention was debated and authorities were questioned whether they had exaggerated the threat from the pandemic (cf. Gherzetti & Odén 2010). There were also criticisms and worries about the economic costs of the vaccination. Overall, there was initial public confidence and trust regarding how the authorities handled the situation. However, in the unfolding of the consequences of the mass-vaccination, the narrative also carried its peripety – an abrupt turn of events and reversal of circumstances. This materialized in reports, starting in the summer of 2010 and continuing during 2011 about children and young people who were diagnosed with the unusual and life-long neurological disease narcolepsy as a side effect of the vaccine (Läkemedelsverket [Medical Products Agency] 2011). For these, now estimated more than 300 young people and their families, the authorities' precautionary measures have turned into personal catastrophes and to alternative pandemic narratives.

Methods

My research project (Epidemics, Vaccination, and the Power of Narratives) started in 2013. That meant, "arriving after the fact" (Fortun 2001: 2), since the pandemic was already over. I began my work in the post-pandemic phase, when the pandemic was officially declared over by the World Health Organization.[2] The Swedish mass-vaccination had passed and the side effects were known. This had of course implications for my study and it is important to remember the different positions of the people involved. For authorities and health professionals the interviews provided situations to look back and reflect on processes and decisions regarding the already past event. The narcolepsy families still faced their problems in the present and in the future.

I carried out my interviews through parallel sessions mostly during 2013 and 2014, with individuals from three groups comprising different formations of the pandemic: 1) authorities, policymakers, and decision-makers, 2) narcolepsy patients and their families, and, 3) health care workers and medical researchers. I have conducted 14 interviews with different officials from authorities, most of them in one way or another connected to the NPG. I have also made 10 interviews with parents of narcoleptic children, and 2 interviews with young adults with narcolepsy. Furthermore, I have made 12 interviews with health care workers and medical researchers. In the citations, the informants are anonymous (as much as it is possible because people in the authorities are often public persons). In the case of the parents, I have used pseudonyms. During the interviews, I have used a person-centered approach (Linger 2005). I started asking the interviewees questions about their childhood, their education and working life. Then the interviews continued with dialogues about experiences of infectious diseases, personal memories of epidemics or pandemics and specific positions during the swine flu pandemic.

In interpreting the interviews my basic tools come from cultural analysis as developed by Ehn and Löfgren (2001) – a critical ethnological approach based on the social and cultural present, but far from leaving history aside. Cultural analysis shows the societal and individual past as part of contemporary ways of living. One of the most important advantages for cultural analysis is its way of creating new forms of understanding and its critical potential for scrutinizing and questioning predominant opinions and dissecting stereotypes and prejudices. Arthur Frank and his method of dialogical narrative analysis also inspired me. Narrative analysis is broadly defined as a method of qualitative research in which the researcher listens to the stories of the research subjects, attempting to understand their experiences, cultural and social framework and the situation at hand (Arvidsson 1998; Riessman 2008). One important element in Arthur Frank's method is the mutual (dialogical) relationship between stories and humans. Stories make life social and connect people into groups and collectivities (Frank 2010: 15). Stories have capacities in many ways – they have the capacity to display characters and to make one particular perspective not only plausible but compelling (Frank 2010: 3). Stories and storytelling also carry inherent morality about what counts as good or bad. Stories are resonant, that is, they echo other stories and sometimes summon up whole cultures (Frank 2010: 37).

In this article, I will focus on two of the interviewee groups. First, my interviews with authorities and policymakers connected to the National Pandemic Group and my interviews with some professionals who in their daily capacities were dependent on the positions taken by the NPG. Interviewing state officials from different authorities implies specific challenges. Legislations, special assignments, specific rationales and organizational limitations frame authorities and their actions. Nevertheless, it is important to note what Didier Fassin has defined as central for an "ethnography of the state", that "the state is a concrete and situated reality ... simultaneously embodied in the individuals and inscribed in a temporality" (Fassin 2013: 4). It is the "agents themselves who make the policy of the state, by feeling more or less constrained by the scope of their job and resources, by taking more or less initiative with respect to the regulations imposed on them" (Fassin 2013: 5).

Some of those I interviewed in the first group were also formal members of the NPG. Their meetings before and during the pandemic have been documented in archived protocols. Maybe due to the ongoing threat from the pandemic together with the Swedish official legislation regarding authorities' documentation (protocols are public and open to any citizen to read), these protocols are quite brief and contain no transcriptions of the discussions or indications of possible disagreements. I studied the protocols after I had made the interviews. Since the interviews provided many nuances regarding the different conditions for taking a stand or making decisions, I read the protocols with curious eyes, to find expressions of doubt and dilemmas.

Second, I will use my findings from interviews with parents of children with narcolepsy and from my participatory observations during some meetings with the NA. These interviews focused on how the side effect had disrupted individual and family lives, but also how patients and parents played an active role in the production of knowledge about narcolepsy and how their ways of forming a collective action has made them create a reflexive organization using collaborative mechanisms, collective action and mutual learning (Rabeharisoa & Callon 2004: 145). In analysing these interview sessions, I had a similar experience as with the NPG interviews. Talking to parents one by one, when they were representing their families or children, provided another kind of information than when asking specifically about the association as the advocating or acting entity. For the association to be able to gain trust both among their members and among medical and governmental authorities it was important for them to navigate strategically between the individual and the organizational levels.

Following Kim Fortun, I define these two constellations (the NPG and the NA) *enunciatory communities*. In Fortun's definition, enunciatory communities make new subject positions emerge as a response to profound change (Fortun 2001: 13). The NPG, although existing since 2005, met a situation of a new and unexpected pandemic that challenged the pre-pandemic preparedness. The families that created the NA had faced a disease that hardly anybody had heard of, and where collective action was necessary. These unexpected realities also involved *double bind* situations – fields of force and contradiction (Fortun 2001: 11), emerging both from the pre-pandemic preparedness and from handling the adverse effect from the mass-vaccination. Double bind situations imply not only difficult choices but also that individuals confront more than one obligation, that could be equally valued, but inconsistent (Fortun 2001: 13). In some cases, the double bind situations could become corroding factors for the chosen strategies.

Advocating Solidarity and Herd Immunity – Strategies, Doubts, and Dilemmas in the National Pandemic Group

The NPG started in 2005 in accordance with WHO proclamations regarding national pandemic preparedness. It played an important role in the Swedish pandemic preparedness and as an actor in European and global networks. The National Board of Health and Welfare (NBHW) was the convening actor, and their Director-General served as the chair of the NPG meetings. Other members in the NPG were the Swedish Institute for Communicable Disease and Control, the Swedish Civil Contingencies Agency, the Swedish Association of Local Authorities and Regions, the Medical Products Agency, the Swedish Work Environment Authority, the National Veterinary Institute, the Swedish Board of Agriculture, and the National Food Agency. During the course of the pandemic, the first four organizations were the most involved with the NPG. The group held their meetings once every week from April to November 2009, after which meetings were less frequent and mostly by teleconferences. The function of the NPG was to support collaboration between all the stakeholders and other actors involved in dealing with the pandemic. Citing Haas (1992: 3), Paul Forster has pointed out both the allure of such collaborative models comprising "epistemic communities" and "communities of shared knowledge" and the simultaneous risk that they might only provide solutions that "support a technical, scientific viewpoint, and exclude others" (Forster 2012: 23).

The specific swine flu accounts in the NPG protocols date back to the spring of 2009. These intensified through September of 2009, and the last protocol concerning the swine flu was on August 11, 2010, the day after the WHO announced that the pandemic was over. Using a person-centred ethnography approach to people in the NPG, broader and sometimes differentiated accounts prevail than can be found in the official protocols. Personalized narratives for analysing the work of the NPG constitute ways of illuminating "how different pathways of responses are created, shaped and justified" (Forster 2012: 4).

The work in the NPG was largely dependent on the previous pandemic preparedness efforts. The preparedness plan before and the evaluations after the swine-flu pandemic and the protocols from the NPG showed that the preparedness was framed by biosecurity together with evidence-based policymaking (see also Holmberg & Lundgren 2016). Biosecurity refers here to the "various technical and political interventions – efforts to 'secure health' – that have been formulated in response to new or newly perceived pathogenic threats" (Lakoff & Collier 2008: 8). Sweden, with its relatively high awareness of biosafety and biosecurity, has implemented a robust and concrete governance, steered by the National Veterinary Institute and the Public Health Agency. One example is the implementation of an internal bio-risk programme, including the high-containment laboratory (BSL-4) at the Public Health Agency of Sweden. This facility is the most advanced in the Nordic countries and one of few in Europe. Other examples are biosecurity and surveillance in animal husbandry and response to effects of so-called invasive species. A third example of Swedish biosecurity is the stockpiling of antivirals in case of influenza pandemics. This area of biosecurity also includes preparedness for mass-vaccination against pandemic spread. All of these examples are related to what Hinchliffe and Bingham have defined as areas of biosecurity (2008: 1535–1536).

Influenza positioned as part of global health security and developed into processes of securitization, have made pandemic declarations matters of national or international security (Buzan 1998). Kezia Barker has argued that this securitization by itself caused a "bureaucratic reflex" when measures were taken during the pandemic (Barker 2012). One example was the Swedish advance purchase agreement with a vaccine supplier and the logistics plans that were in place for distributing the vaccine. When the WHO declared phase 6 of the pandemic, the purchase agreement was enacted and the vaccine was produced and distributed (MSB & Socialstyrelsen 2011).

Thus, the swine flu experience represented the first "real-life test" of pandemic preparedness after the NPG started in 2005. Briggs and Hallin (2016: 120) also accentuate the pandemic as a primary real-life test in their analysis of how previous communication exercises came back as realities in 2009. Reading the protocols from the NPG is a way to recognize how each statement, although shortened by bureaucratic language, iterates "nested worlds" that implicate each other in specific ways. The protocols form a chain of arguments combining health security and evidence-based practice with certain core categories and strategies. These include the special characteristics of the H1N1 pandemic, the assessment of who was at risk, the concept of herd immunity, trust in the evidence for vaccination, the mass-vaccination intervention, the strategic use of the solidarity argument, and the importance of consensus regarding measures and information. As we will see, the interviews provide important nuances to this picture.

The risk assessment was based on experiences from previous pandemics and seasonal influenza outbreaks as well as the reported pandemic outcome during the summer of 2009 from Mexico, the United States, and the southern hemisphere. The reports stated that children and young people were especially afflicted (MSB & Socialstyrelsen 2011: 9). The facts about afflicted children would eventually lead to somewhat confusing information from the authorities. Although young people were not considered a medical risk groups, the NBHW designed a special Facebook-campaign to reach the young adults for vaccination.

The social, cultural, and historical context – Sweden as a modern Scandinavian welfare society with a historically high degree of institutional trust and several experiences with successful medical and public health interventions – is important to have in mind. The formal structure with a division between the governmental level and the self-government by counties and municipalities is another essential condition. The county councils made the formally operative decisions concerning for example the mass-vaccination. As a part of the Swedish constitution, this principle of local self-government (*kommunala självstyret*) gives the county councils the right to design and structure their activities concerning public health. However, in practice, there were strong limitations regarding the possibilities to act in other ways than the pandemic plans had proposed.

Sweden has had a long history of vaccination practices and a very high coverage in the national child vaccination programme. Even voluntary seasonal flu vaccinations had a relatively high uptake during the years prior to the swine flu pandemic (http://www.socialstyrelsen.se/publikationer2013/2013-6-37). The ways officials talk about child vaccination as a success story in medical history, resemble what Rabinow and Rose define as a hybridized truth, mixing biology, susceptibility, and demography (Rabinow & Rose 2006: 197). This perception also characterized pandemic vaccination interventions. Although there were reports indicating that there was no conclusive evidence for the effectiveness of previous seasonal influenza vaccines for the elderly[3], pandemic mass-vaccination was considered the best preventive measure. There was no evidence for the efficacy of the new vaccine, or for the risks of severe side effects. A special fast-track procedure was established for the new pandemic vaccine, with the European Medical Agency as responsible main actor.

In hindsight, commenting on the mass-vaccination and the serious side effect of narcolepsy, one official at the NBHW recalled:

Vaccination is fundamentally the best intervention to prevent a disease … the tragic outcome of the pandemic with narcolepsy is very tragic and deeply sad. Nevertheless, all the critics, they are now looking at this *a posteriori*, in hindsight, and of course then it is easy to have an answer. Nevertheless, when you are to judge a situation where people, young people, children, died in the southern hemisphere, where the intensive care units were inundated by influenza patients… That's what is interesting now in the global world, the rest of the world can sit on the balcony and plan what to do because we know it will come to us. (Interview with official at the NBHW, February 27, 2013)

The concept of "herd immunity" was articulated together with "solidarity" in the communication about the mass-vaccination and was emphasized as an important constituent part in the argumentation in favour of the vaccine intervention. The arguments aimed to persuade people to accept vaccination as an altruistic way to protect those who for different reasons could not take the vaccine. The argumentations turned out to be a mixture of a political strategy and of epidemiological evidence.

While proclaiming vaccination as a rational and reasonable decision for all, there were no arguments regarding categories such as ethnicity, gender, or religion. Also, there were no special arguments regarding specific ways of communicating with different hard-to-reach groups, for example, homeless people, refugees or ethnic minorities. However, the official recommendation for vaccination was translated into 18 different languages. In the informal group "Pandemic analysis" at the National Board of Health and Welfare, specific discussions were held about the risk of forgetting some groups in society. Were there enough efforts made to get sufficient knowledge and reach all minority groups in Sweden? My impression is that these discussions did not become part of the agenda of the NPG, although the issues were brought to their attention (personal communication with formal official at NBHW). One official of the NPG explained to me some of the reasons for claiming the solidarity argument:

Yes, in this case, there was a very strong solidarity argument because the experiences from the southern hemisphere indicated that this was a very serious disease. … And it was the fact that you do it for yourself, but just as much for your family and friends and the weakest in society. Actually, this is the first time, as far as I can remember, that we have had a solidarity argument, that it became such a foundational argument for this. … I think it is really interesting that solidarity could be such a foundation… I think it was correct. Because most of those who would have been afflicted, the children, had no say in the matter… (Interview with official at the NBHW, February 27, 2013)

This quote emphasizes solidarity as an important argument for the mass-vaccination, although it does not confirm its use generally in public health. As I will argue later, there are different interpretations of whether solidarity has its base in public health work or in national state politics, or in both.

Consensus vs. Doubts and Dilemmas
The NPG protocols of 2009 and 2010 are rather brief and describe no contradictions, no questionings, and no inner conflicts. When reading them after I had made the interviews, I was somewhat surprised to learn about the outspoken consensus. The first protocol in 2009 (April 28) explicitly stated the need for consensus with "to agree upon", "to co-ordinate", "to voice in common", "to having press conferences in common", etc. It is repeatedly expressed in the protocol that the NPG shared the WHO's judgments and recommendations. The Ministry of Health and Social Affairs also communicated to the NPG that "all information needs to be unanimous" and "that the experts must follow those agreements about messages that the information officers have been involved in bringing forward" (quote from NPG protocol May 5, 2009). This indicates how restricted this epistemic community was, and actually was designed to be.

One official commented on the consensus in the interview:

Obviously, you can never have a one hundred percent consensus for a measure as large as this one [*the mass-vaccination*]. However, in the NPG, we had full consensus. (Interview with official at the NBHW, February 27, 2013)

Still, the official talks of at least one person, who afterwards has claimed an opposing opinion regarding the mass-vaccination, but never voiced during the meetings:

And that was really the fact, and that is interesting, that he afterwards spoke in a way that I don't think anyone should: "I regret I did not oppose it." Because he never opposed it in the NPG. What he said at the time in the NPG was all about frustration in not getting the vaccine quickly enough. Therefore, his change of heart has come very conveniently afterwards. He had every opportunity to question this during every weekly meeting. (Interview with official at the NBHW, February 27, 2013)

Later, I interviewed the particular official who was criticized. I asked him how he felt about the vaccination intervention, and he told me he had doubts during the pandemic. His opinion was that medical decisions are not always rational, but rather influenced by psychological mechanisms, for example, people being scared that showing doubt would risk the much-desired national consensus that was considered the best course of action.

It is this interesting psychology … Why don't people speak more about this? I discussed this with some colleagues, and it turned out that many were quite hesitant. But it is that psychological mechanism. (Interview with official at the Swedish Association of Local Authorities and Regions], March 8, 2013)

He concluded that it was a wrong decision to take, not because of fear of side effects, that were considered very unlikely, but because he considered evidence indicating that the pandemic would not strike as hard as predicted.

We knew from Australia … that about 10 percent of the population would be ill. That turned out to be true. … We knew that this pandemic differed from the seasonal flu in two respects, the older were largely immune, and that is where the biggest risk groups are. This was also shown. We knew that we had some scary cases among young people. In fact, we assessed very precise data. We have always said that you should vaccinate everyone if there is 30–40 percent risk of falling ill. We knew it would be 10 percent, yet we chose to vaccinate everyone. It is quite irrational.

My interviews with different officials were ways of making "second-order observations", meaning that I tried to observe what my interviewees observed, according to Niklas Luhmann's terminology (Caduff 2014b; Luhmann 1998). As Carlo Caduff has suggested, the focus on experts and their reasoning risks replicating "biosecurity's ideology of efficiency and rationality" (Caduff 2014a: 8.4). This is very much the case, but this official's remarks on what is rational or not, still reveal some tensions and contradictions concerning aspects of biosecurity. Governments and authorities with the responsibility to protect people face double-edged challenges or fears. One is the fear of having done too little and afterwards being accused of having disregarded the threat and thereby causing unnecessary damage. "There is always a political imperative to be seen to be doing something in the era of anxiety, worry and perceived threat" (Scoones 2010: 149). The other fear is overreaction, "crying wolf" and to be accused of wasting money and trust. Behind these fears, there is also an underlying worry to lose control and be outflanked and powerless facing epidemics. This situation of "damned if you do and damned if you don't" can explain why it was possible to simultaneously argue both that the pandemic would be severe and that it would be mild.

The official in the above quote also commented on the political involvement and, at times, the political interrelations with the medical expertise in the policy- and decision-making procedures. In August, the Ministry of Health and Social Affairs created a special informal group including the National Board of Health and Welfare, the Swedish Institute for Communicable Disease Control, the Swedish Civil Contingencies Agency, and the Swedish Association of Local Authorities and Regions. This group was also described in the evaluation report (MSB & Socialstyrelsen 2011). The aim was "a political group as a complementary group to the NPG" (protocol August 25, 2009). This group should "synchronize the authorities' and the government's work and their public messages". The Ministry took over the responsibility of handling the press conferences from September 1 and onwards. New routines unfolded. Up until then, there were press conferences only when something new had occurred. Now they were to be held every week at a fixed time and place.

Some officials also argued that politicians claimed the solidarity argument. One official remembered the meetings that the prime minister had with his council for crisis management, where the political representatives had stated that they would not accept that anyone should die in Sweden when you could vaccinate against it. Moreover, this vaccine was intended to the whole population (Interview with official at the European Centre for Disease Prevention and Control, February 28, 2013).

Another official also declared that the solidarity principle came from the politicians. This was an official guideline because of the previously mentioned separation between the national health authorities and the county councils. However, the solidarity argument was also discussed actively and independently in the main convening authority National Board of Health and Welfare (personal communication with former official at the NBHW).

These examples show that both the public health authorities and the politicians were highly engaged in propagating the mass-vaccination for the "whole population". The Swedish nation was the targeted collective for both public health and state politics. Consequently, the political collaboration with the expert authorities made it possible to make science a component of politics and to motivate political interests and aims (Haas 1990: 11; Kamradt-Scott 2012: S118). Thus, an interrelation between solidarity as a political argument and herd immunity as a medical and epidemiological argument arose.

Was the political involvement a double bind situation for the NPG? This involvement in the expert authorities' agenda implied that experts and officials became influenced by, or obliged to pay loyalties to, the political demands. If, from the standpoints of their own professions, from their personal convictions, or from evidence-based argumentations, they concluded differently than the politicians about what was the right thing to do, they were clearly in a double bind situation, because agreeing with the politicians meant giving up on their own knowledge or expertise-position. This double bind would add one more risk besides the one that Forster has pointed out – that communities of shared experiences will only propagate narrow technical solutions. In this case, the political involvement made visible by, for example, performative utterances at press conferences, etc., about solidarity and the "whole population" was at odds with some of the NPG members' professional or evidence-based practices and experiences in handling influenza epidemics. On the other hand, the weekly press conferences, framed by politicians, also said something about the pragmatics of biopolitical communication (Briggs 2009: 191). Although the different authorities involved realized the risk that journalists would tire of press conferences with no actual news, the health authorities also saw an opportunity to make themselves visible to the public and to make their competences broadly known.

The double bind also made itself obvious for some key professionals in the course of the pandemic even if they were not directly involved in the NPG. Signs of doubt came from three doctors and a journalist who criticized the vaccine purchase agreement in one of the leading Swedish newspapers (*Svenska Dagbladet,* October 6, 2009). The article argued that the influenza pandemic would not be severe, and yet authorities had put great emphasis on solidarity. They continued by arguing that this was a solidarity for the already rich because the purchase agreement placed Sweden ahead of poorer countries in the global distribution of vaccines. Because the agreement contained secret paragraphs, it was not transparent enough to make it obvious who would be responsible if there were severe adverse effects from the vaccine.

A Swedish paediatrician, who for many years had been involved in child immunization programs, also had worries about the vaccination of children and the quality and safety of the vaccine. She knew that she would have to comply with a decision about mass-vaccination, but she wanted to know more of the facts. She wrote a letter to all the director generals who were members of the NPG.

> If we are going to mass-vaccinate children, we need to have better knowledge about the basic data. I demanded that an expert meeting should be held to be able to find out what was in the vaccine. (Interview March 7, 2013)

The protocol of the NPG on August 25, 2009, also mentions her wish for the meeting. She wanted all the international experts available but was told this was too expensive. She remained worried about the adjuvant in the vaccine:

> At the same time, because I was worried, I went out and tried to find out about the adjuvant … and I found out that this is a substance used all over the world in health food stores where they claim it can cure cancer and strengthen your immune defence, or whatever. Nothing indicated it would be dangerous, but it was not tested on children. … At the same time, we had this threat.

She was very eager to tell me about her way of *balancing* facts.

> This was in the summer – August or September … I was forced to find all this out for myself and I was interviewed on television in the autumn. I remember the most important thing for me was, "Would I be able to recommend this to my children and grandchildren?" I really made great efforts in finding information. On the one hand, it was the adjuvant, which was a bit scary. The other was the information that was brought forward

about the influenza. We had contacts with Australia and with London and we should inform every nurse in Stockholm. Before doing that, I had to take a stand. …. And we *weighed together* all the data we had from Australia that told us that this is dangerous. From London, we had data from July. Children *died! Children* died! And not only "at-risk children". And I tried to weigh it all together, and finally could say to myself … Yes, I can recommend this to my children and grandchildren – while at the same time there was a worry. (Interview March 7, 2013)

She told me she wanted to start a "worry group". "If you are going to vaccinate this many children, why not have all the experts in for a hearing? … But still, you probably wouldn't have known about narcolepsy anyway." She made a PowerPoint presentation and held lectures for vaccinators, doctors, and nurses based on her results of balancing and weighing different kinds of information. Being trapped in a situation where a pandemic was unfolding in real-time (Caduff 2010: 213), she felt sufficiently secure. However, on her way home from work one day the next summer, she saw a newspaper headline about the initial narcolepsy reports.

Frankly speaking, Hell! What is this? It felt like a stranglehold! Is this really true? (Interview March 7, 2013)

Phrasing it as a stranglehold meant that the main purpose of the mass-vaccination – to protect people's lives and health – had backfired into something completely unexpected. This serious side effect, particularly hitting young people, would risk putting a definitive stop for containment measures of that kind during influenza pandemics. The side effect could also result in a backlash for the previously so successful child immunization programme. Her wish was that the reports would not be true and that these adverse reactions would eventually turn out to have another cause than the vaccine.

Even health authorities in general were sceptic to the news and a long procedure started for the afflicted young people to get their symptoms diagnosed as narcolepsy and to prove that the disease was an effect of the vaccine (Lundgren 2015b).

Advocating Social Justice in the Association for Narcolepsy

Narcolepsy is a serious and debilitating chronic neurological condition, characterized by excessive daytime sleep, cataplexies, hypnagogic hallucinations, sleep paralyses and also learning disabilities, depression, obesity and disturbed metabolism. The disease is lifelong and there is no existing cure, only symptomatic relief from different kinds of medication for sleeping disorder and cataplexies, and central stimulants for sleepiness (see Lundgren 2015b).

The NA was formed in 2010 in response to the narcolepsy cases that resulted from vaccination with Pandemrix. Rather than joining the national neurological patient organization, the parents of the diseased children started a new association. The members of the association came from all over the country, with the majority from the south and middle of Sweden. The board meetings were held mostly through telephone meetings and during some family gatherings every year. As described elsewhere (Lundgren 2015b), their work can be summarized as a quest for social justice in their fight to influence researchers and decision-makers to find a cure or a treatment, in their struggles for economic compensation for the narcoleptic children, and in their work to build networks, share knowledge, and provide support to afflicted families (www.narkolepsiföreningen.se). They have also played an important role for the development of narcolepsy research in Sweden. As a concerned group, through intermediary representatives, they have searched for affiliations with research collectives, and thereby broadened the scope for new scientific problematizations (cf. Callon, Lascoumes & Barthe 2011: 87). Their critical narratives about the mass-vaccination and the lack of state culpability that they experience have been enacted as performances for justice in public spaces as well as in the media and in political meetings (Lundgren 2015b). Their voices have come to represent the experiences that pre-pandemic preparedness and earlier evidence-based practice deemed very unthinkable, or an unknown unknown (Kerwin 1993: 178) – a serious side effect, particularly one afflicting young people.

Although the association dates formally back to 2010, the individual narratives start from their respective vaccination decisions and will probably continue at least as long as the children who have the disease are around to tell them. In many cases, the stories go back to a time before the vaccination, when the children were well and healthy and the disease that would strike them was impossible to anticipate in their minds.

Even if the interviews show cracks in the consensus, members of the NPG and other actors often spoke clearly of the inherent qualities of health policies, of vaccination in general as a success story, and of the importance of taking responsibility for the Swedish population as a whole, as well as for the specific groups that were at risk. Some talked about their own subjective experiences of infectious diseases and about their parents' generation when vaccination as a preventive measure started to be available for everyone. Their basic trust in medicine and in medical knowledge was evident.

Not surprisingly, the parents of the narcoleptic children did not share these opinions, but instead presented different kinds of critical narratives while at the same time emphasizing the positive qualities of the association, the parents, and the children. In addition, the pandemic preparedness itself was criticized. One of the parents rather cynically commented on the NPG:

> The NPG was put together in relation to the avian flu; they needed something to play with. And they found something, the swine flu virus, and they went ahead... (Interview with Cecil, December 7, 2012)

Several parents were also very critical about the arguments of solidarity and of herd immunity that had made them feel emotionally trapped. Their vaccination decisions arose both out of solidarity with those who could not take the vaccine and because they wanted to protect their own children against a disease that was said to hit young people especially severely (Lundgren 2015b; Lundgren 2016). Ironically, it was the children, young adults and the middle-aged persons that authorities feared would get the swine flu in its most severe form. This is why they also put much emphasis on young people to vaccinate. The reports after the pandemic have shown that the incidence of laboratory-confirmed cases of the flu was highest among children, and the number of cases decreased with increasing age (Smittskyddsinstitutet 2011).

The parents' stories were about the different difficulties that the families so suddenly were faced with (Frank 2010: 28), but the stories were also largely about morals, guilt and issues of responsibility. The emotional content was apparent in all the interviews, in their different ways of presenting what Anne Hunsaker Hawkins has labelled "angry pathographies". They presented critical opinions about the cause of the disease, claiming political reasons for their illness. They were also critical regarding health professionals, politicians, and what one should expect from the state but did not receive ("the moral culpability of the state") (Hunsaker Hawkins 1999: 128; Trundle & Scott 2013: 503). Some also criticized the use of the solidarity argument and the Swedish obedience to the health politics of the WHO and the EU.

The parents (for example Peter and Cecil) both used very lively and expressive language in knitting together the story of the pandemic with this critique of politicians, authorities, and decision-makers and even of Swedish culture as a whole. Peter defined himself as always "ambivalent towards group behaviour" and contrasted this with a description of Swedish culture as an "army of people thinking the same way" (interview with Peter, May 20, 2013). Peter's narrative formulated a strong critique rooted in his opinion that authorities had overreacted to the pandemic threat and underreacted when it came to taking responsibility for the people who suffered from the effects of the bad decisions about the need for mass-vaccination. They directed their anger towards the lack of responsible action from authorities and politicians. Peter compared this with other state institutions that he also criticized for having lost their trustworthiness. He warned about the breakdown of the welfare state while at the same time its citizens were unaware of what was happening – "we are not sceptical enough, we are too credulous and simple-minded". He concluded by stating:

> Sweden is most badly hit because we deserve it... we need to have more integrity. Every day we are manipulated... Go on and make a Hollywood movie about that! (Interview with Peter, May 20, 2013)

While speaking about narcolepsy, the parents also spoke about character, including their children's and their own and that of other actors. Experiencing trauma, injustice, and a persistent struggle for support and compensation led to uniform descriptions of "the other", in this case "authorities", "politicians", or "doctors". The characterizations of individuals in these groups seldom escaped the stereotypes. Instead, they remained indistinct but still powerful or even dictatorial. These descriptions also shaped the self-identity of the suffering community as being made up of well-defined and worried parents and knowledge-seeking and responsible citizens.

The stories were strong, often heart-breaking, and informed about what was perceived as good or bad, about how to behave, and what is deplorable (Frank 2010: 36). The inherent morality was shown, for example, in the choice of words. "Authorities only say blah-blah", Peter said, and he went on saying, "In ten years' time the scandal and the violation will be obvious." He used the word "injection-plants" (*injiceringsanläggningar*) to describe the vaccination stations and made a morbid joke saying, "it was almost like gas chambers being established within a very short time" to describe the mass-vaccination at workplaces and hospitals. He was critical of the mass-vaccination effort when the flu had already reached its peak – like "giving artificial respiration when the patient is already dead" (interview with Peter, May 20, 2013). By linking his story to a lack of state culpability, he argued in favour of a political etiology as an explanatory cause of the side effect, interacting with the biomedical etiology no matter the definition of the latter – whether as genetic disposition, the vaccine adjuvant, or the virus itself. Expressions of cynicism and mistrust were also apparent regarding what parents considered as the bureaucratic reductionism played out in different authorities' guidelines in handling the narcolepsy. Strict and formal guidelines were implemented in testing each individual's disease progression to determine if there was an obligation to provide state support. The issue of the state's lack of moral culpability ran through all interviews with the parents. In some stories, the critique contained recognition of the state's good intentions and the unfortunate events that occurred in the process of the pandemic and the vaccination intervention. According to most parents, the remaining responsibility of the state and the politicians was to secure whatever was left of trust by giving sufficient support to the patients (cf. Trundle 2011: 887). Another kind of critique apparent in the interviews was more radical and placed authorities and politicians alongside biomedical agents as *primary causes* for the suffering. This critique was directed against the different intersecting power structures no matter whether they were derived from the state, the biomedical community, or from the corporate interests that offered or denied resources for recognition and legitimation (cf. Trundle & Scott 2013: 512).

Elsewhere, I have shown that the NA besides being critical and seeking justice also took great responsibility in collaborations with researchers, with authorities, and with politicians (Lundgren 2015b). In addition to speaking of how authorities had exaggerated the pandemic and that the side effect was caused by profit-seeking big pharma and corrupt researchers, they worked with the problems in ways characterized by reflective consciousness.

Enunciatory Communities – Politics and Ethics for the Future

In 2017, eight years have passed since the pandemic outbreak and the mass-vaccination. The NA still continuously reports that they receive new members. The Pharmaceutical Insurance (Svenska Läkemedelsförsäkringen) has previously established 8 months as the time limit for documented side effects after the vaccination. In an update report in 2016, the limit was extended to 24 months.[4] Some researchers have even begun discussing the possibility of a "second hit" of narcolepsy if people vaccinated with Pandemrix get an infection or something else that could trigger the immune system into an autoimmune reaction (comment from a medical expert during a meeting with the NA, medical experts and public health officials at the Sahlgrenska University Hospital in Gothenburg, April 3, 2014).

My interviews together with biomedical research confirm the high rate of medical disablement that comes with the disease (Vetenskapsrådet 2012). The disease also affects social relations, sexuality, working life, economy and the general sense of well-being. The main administrative problem for the families during 2017 is the process of judging the criteria for assessing invalidity for the narcoleptics. Insurance Sweden and its Committee for Insurance of Persons has proposed an invalidity rate from 5% to 20% (which is the same as if a person has lost half or a whole thumb).[5] The NA is protesting against the proposal and the outcome of this issue is still unknown. This procedure is the latest of a long range of administrative, long-during painstaking processes that the families have undergone since 2009, all of which have demanded tremendous patience.

The collected ethnography from the NPG shows both the unanimousness of the strategies in upholding core categories such as solidarity and herd immunity, and some obvious doubts, dilemmas, and double bind situations. It is not easy to know if these situations would have been recognized if the side effects had not occurred. The narcolepsy side effect could very well turn out to be the strongest corroding factor for the chosen strategy of mass-vaccination – but the fact that the pandemic eventually turned out to be milder than expected was also an undermining factor. The mildness of the pandemic could be verified early in the process (cf. Caduff 2010: 213), but the side effect was only possible to observe in retrospect.

The struggles and strategies in the NA also point to dilemmas and double bind situations in their advocacy for social justice. In fact, the very creation of the association in response to a vaccine-caused disease is a consequence of the double bind described earlier: decisions derived from political imperatives about solidarity and expert authorities and medical professionals' devotion to evidence-based policy and practice. The common-sense argument about mass-vaccination that was established was a way to combine these two concepts, although many doubts and dilemmas remained. Some members of the association clearly have gone on the offensive against medical authorities and politicians, while others have chosen a path following a strategy of collaboration with authorities and medical experts (Lundgren 2015b).

During 2014, the association formulated its statement of opinion regarding a governmental proposal on economic compensation for the afflicted patients. This instance was one example when the differences between the strategies were handled as an asset. Rather than forcing one single unanimous answer, the association arranged a meeting where parents could formulate their personal opinions, resulting in many different opinions forwarded as statements. In this particular case, the pluralism and the multi-vocal responses to the government was accepted as a strategy for the association and as evidence of individually competent and responsible parents (Field notes from a gathering with the association, September 26–28, 2014). What would be the corroding factors for the advocacy performed by the NA? One factor that was sometimes mentioned both with anger and with fear was that of using a *genetic* disposition as a prerequisite for getting narcolepsy as an argument against state culpability. The specific genotypes that are found in almost 100% of the narcoleptic patients are also common in the Swedish population (20%–30%). Still, narcolepsy is a very rare disease. Although medical research is clear about the vaccine's role in the rise of incidence, some parents or young people have met the argument that "you would have gotten narcolepsy later on anyway". For the advocating association, such an argument risks undermining the collectivizing efforts that constitute their politics and instead push the patients and the disease into individualized positions (Rabinow & Rose 2006: 215).

The two enunciatory communities represent different aspects of "temporal incongruity" (Caduff 2014b: 302). As Caduff argues, pre-pandemic experts are often ruled by the so-called precautionary principle: "prepare for the worst and hope for the best". This precaution also enables actors to "commit a leap of faith" to have trust in a particular kind of future and to intervene even if there is not a full understanding of the risks in question (Caduff 2014b: 302). Caduff concludes: "Faced with an unknown future and uncertain probability calculation, the decision to proceed and intervene becomes an eminently political one, even if it does not appear as such" (Caduff 2014b: 303).

For the NA, the temporal incongruity was of another kind. They contemplated their own decisions made while balancing supposed "known knowns" (influenza could be life threatening), and maybe worrying about "unknown knowns" (virus can mutate into even more dangerous forms), but not fearing "unknown unknowns" (side effects that were unthinkable) (cf. Kerwin 1993; Braun 2007: 18; Leung & Nicoll 2010). Their position afterwards, as both the subject and object of the unknown unknowns, has put them into a specific ethical position. Elsewhere, I have discussed the state of political invisibility that the families have experienced (Lundgren 2016). The side effect was unexpected, unwelcome, and almost unthinkable. The disease and talk of the disease has made the invisibility of side effects from influenza vaccination evolve into visibility. What the narcoleptic families often experience is that authorities or actors of the state re-manufacture invisibility through silence and defense or shift the focus from the health effects to economic costs and administrative problems (cf. Beck 2016: 101). This causes hidden spaces of unwanted circumstances, "a production of margins", as Seljemaa and Siim have formulated it in their introductory article about silence and silencing (2016: 6). The mass-vaccination was intended to be an act both of compassion (expressed as solidarity), and of containment (of the epidemic to reach herd immunity). However, the families experience the "*containment of themselves*, their removal into an unwanted space of societal failure and paradoxical feelings of shame and guilt" (Lundgren 2016: 1112). As I have argued, the fragmentation or muting of the side effect – also if it is placed within specific national domains – will reduce the cosmopolitical potentials for pandemic preparedness and response. Looking at it from another angle, this actual side effect could in fact enable a possibility to create strengthened reflexive awareness, which in turn can strengthen public trust regarding possible future interventions (Lundgren 2017).

Although the narratives from the two enunciatory communities run in parallel, they differ in almost every way in their histories of inception, their ways of working, and their agendas. They share one important characteristic – they are both "performing ethics in anticipation of the future" (Fortun 2001: 16). This is obvious in their ways of handling the knowledge of the past to shape and legitimate certain strategies for the future. In this articulation of ethics, solidarity and responsibility are important sense-making categories for both groups, although used in separate ways.

According to Fortun, the differences within enunciatory communities are resources rather than problems (Fortun 2001: 13). In the NPG, it is obvious that differences were a problem and a threat to the group's strategy and activities. If the goal for the future is to create more usable tools in participatory preparatory work preceding decision-making and implementation, the NPG needs to take seriously, what Sheila Jasanoff has called the four "technologies of humility". These would be *framing* of the problem, assessing *vulnerability*, analysing the *distribution* of technology, and *learning*, "through which societies can collectively reflect on the ambiguity of their experiences" (Jasanoff 2003: 238 ff.).

In 2017 eight years have passed, but the H1N1 pandemic is still "produced, suffered, and remembered" (cf. Fortun 2001: 6). While looking at the national implications of influenza in relation to global biological complexes (e.g. Braun 2007; Dehner 2012) the works of Paul Rabinow and Nikolas Rose are important. Their definition of biopower, with elements such as truth discourses, strategies for intervention and modes of subjectification (Rabinow & Rose 2006: 97), is certainly applicable to the work within the National Pandemic Group. However, the argumentations put forward by Bruce Braun (2007) and Sujatha Raman and Richard Tutton (2010: 728) in defining biopolitics as something broader, that also include "a multiple politics with inequalities, opportunities, complexities, and dilemmas both individually and collectively", require a more nuanced exploration (Raman & Tutton 2010: 730). This is important because such a standpoint makes way for collectivity and "the complex links between power-from-above and power-from-below" (2010: 728). The complex links that are discernible in the juxtaposition of these two enunciatory communities provide necessary tools for future pandemic preparedness and response. These tools are for example the different interpretations of solidarity. On the one side solidarity is an emotional actor involved in preventive measures taken from public health authorities and from politicians. On the other side, its emotional power is an argument for social justice from the NA. Another tool is the use of ethnography and reflexive dialogues as ways to explore doubts and dilemmas, that otherwise are hidden from official declarations (Lundgren 2017). If taken into account, this study would not only be contributing to some of the uncomfortable truths that Atlani-Duault and Carl Kendall asked for in their article (2009) in the early phase of the pandemic, but also to suggestions for handling them.

Notes

1 I want to express my gratitude to the Marcus and Amalia Wallenberg Foundation for granting this project and to all my informants whom I have interviewed. Ethics approval was from the Regional Ethical Review Board, May 29, 2012 (dnr 2012-133-31).
2 http://www.who.int/csr/disease/swineflu/phase/en/.
3 www.cochrane.org/CD004876/ARI_vaccines-for-preventing-seasonal-influenza-and-its-complications-in-people-aged-65-or-older.
4 http://lff.se/wp-content/uploads/2016/07/Pandemrix-och-narkolepsi-uppdatering-13.pdf.
5 http://www.narkolepsiforeningen.se/assets/files/narkolepsi-tabellverk-remiss-161211.pdf.

References

Arvidsson, Alf 1998: *Livet som berättelse: Studier i levnadshistoriska intervjuer*. Lund: Studentlitteratur.
Atlani-Duault, Laëtitia & Carl Kendall 2009: Influenza, Anthropology, and Global Uncertainties. *Medical Anthropology* 28:3, 207–211.
Barker, Kezia 2012: Influenza Preparedness and the Bureaucratic Reflex: Anticipating and Generating the 2009 H1N1 Event. *Health & Place* 18, 701–709.
Beck, Ulrich 2016: *The Metamorphosis of the World*. Cambridge: Cambridge Polity Press.
Braun, Bruce 2007: Biopolitics and the Molecularization of Life. *Cultural Geographies* 14, 6–28.
Briggs, Charles 2009: Biocommunicability and the Biopolitics of Pandemic Threats. *Medical Anthropology* 28:3, 189–198.
Briggs, Charles L. & Daniel C. Hallin 2016: *Making Health Public: How News Coverage is Remaking Media, Medicine, and Contemporary Life*. London & New York: Routledge.
Buzan, Barry 1998: *Security: A New Framework for Analysis*. Boulder, Colorado: Lynne Rienner Pub.
Caduff, Carlo 2010: Public Prophylaxis: Pandemic Influenza, Pharmaceutical Prevention and Participatory Governance. *BioSocieties* 5:2, 199–218.
Caduff, Carlo 2014a: On the Verge of Death: Visions of Biological Vulnerability. *Annual Review of Anthropology* 43:8, 8.1–8.17.
Caduff, Carlo 2014b: Pandemic Prophecy, or How to Have Faith in Reason. *Current Anthropology* 55:3, 296–315.
Callon Michel, Pierre Lascoumes & Yannick Barthe 2011: *Acting in an Uncertain World: An Essay on Technical Democracy*. Cambridge, Massachusetts & London: MIT Press.
Dehner, George 2012: *Global Flu and You: A History of Influenza*. London: Reaktion Books.
Ehn, Billy & Orvar Löfgren 2001: *Kulturanalyser*. 2 ed. Lund: Gleerups.
Farmer, Paul 1999: *Infection and Inequalities: The Modern Plagues*. Berkeley: University of California Press.
Fassin, Didier 2013: Governing Precarity. In: D. Fassin et al., *At the Heart of the State: The Moral World of Institutions*. London: Pluto Press, pp. 1–11.
Forster, Paul 2012: To Pandemic or Not? Reconfiguring Global Responses to Influenza. *STEPS Working Paper* 51. Brighton: STEPS Centre.
Fortun, Kim 2001: *Advocacy after Bhopal: Environmentalism, Disaster, New Global Orders*. Chicago & London: The University of Chicago Press.

Frank, Arthur W. 2010: *Letting Stories Breathe: A Socio-Narratology*. Chicago & London: The University of Chicago Press.

Gherzetti, Marina & Tomas A. Odén 2010: *Pandemin som kom av sig: Om svininfluensan i medier och opinion*. Göteborg: Institutionen för journalistik, medier och kommunikation.

Haas, Ernst B. 1990: *When Knowledge is Power: Three Models of Change in International Organizations*. London: University of California Press.

Haas, Peter M. 1992: Epistemic Communities and International Policy Coordination. *International Organizations* 46:1, 1–35.

Hinchliffe, Steve & Nick Bingham 2008: Securing Life: The Emerging Practices of Biosecurity. *Environment and Planning A*, 40, 1534–1551.

Holmberg, Martin 2016: The Ghost of Pandemics Past: Revisiting Two Centuries of Influenza in Sweden. *Medical Humanities* doi: 101136/medhum-2016-01102.

Holmberg, Martin & Britta Lundgren 2016: Framing Post-Pandemic Preparedness – Comparing Eight European Plans. *Global Public Health* http://dx.doi.org/10.1080/17441692.2016.1149202.

Hunsaker Hawkins, Anne 1999: Pathography: Patient Narratives of Illness. *Culture and Medicine* 171, 127–129.

Jasanoff, Sheila 2003: Technologies of Humility: Citizen Participation in Governing Science. *Minerva* 41, 223–244.

Kamradt-Scott, Adam 2012: Evidence-Based Medicine and the Governance of Pandemic Influenza. *Global Public Health* 7, S2, S111–S126.

Kerwin, Ann 1993: None Too Solid: Medical Ignorance. *Science Communication* 15, 166–185.

Läkemedelsverket (Medical Products Agency) 2011: Occurrence of Narcolepsy with Cataplexy among Children and Adolescents in Relation to the H1N1 Pandemic and Pandemrix Vaccinations. Results of a case inventory study by the MPA in Sweden during 2009–2010, http://www.lakemedelsverket.se/upload/nyheter/2011/Fallinventeringsrapport_pandermrix_110630.pdf.

Lakoff, Andrew 2008: The Generic Biothreat, or How We Became Unprepared. *Cultural Anthropology* 3:3, 399–428.

Lakoff, Andrew & Stephen J. Collier 2008: Biosecurity Interventions: Global Health and Security in Question. New York: Columbia University Press.

Leung, Gabriel M. & Angus Nicoll 2010: Reflections on Pandemic (H1N1) 2009 and the International Response. *PLoS Med* Oct. 2010, 7:10, e1000346. Published online Oct. 5, 2010, doi: 10.1371/journal.pmed.1000346.

Linger, Daniel Tuoro 2005: *Anthropology through a Double Lens: Public and Personal Worlds in Human Theory*. Philadelphia: University of Pennsylvania Press.

Luhmann, Niklas 1998: *Observations on Modernity*. Stanford, CA: Stanford Univ. Press.

Lundgren, Britta 2013: En pandemis vetenskapliga verkligheter. *Kulturella Perspektiv* 1, 21–24.

Lundgren, Britta 2015a: Medicinsk humaniora – en arena för utmaning och experiment. *Kulturella Perspektiv* 1, 2–10.

Lundgren, Britta 2015b: Narrating Narcolepsy – Centering a Side Effect. *Medical Anthropology* 34:2, 150–165.

Lundgren, Britta 2015c: 'Rhyme or Reason?' Saying no to Mass Vaccination: Subjective Re-Interpretation in the Context of the A (H1N1) Influenza Pandemic in Sweden 2009–2010. *Medical Humanities* 41:2, 107–112.

Lundgren, Britta 2015d: The Common Cold, Influenza and Immunity in Post-Pandemic Times – Lay Representation of Self and Other among Older People in Sweden. *Health, Culture, and Society* 8:2, 46–59.

Lundgren, Britta 2016: Solidarity at the Needle Point – the Intersection of Compassion and Containment during the A (H1N1) Pandemic in Sweden 2009. *Sociology and Anthropology* 4:12, 1108–1116.

Lundgren, Britta 2017: Impact, genomslag eller värdeskapande – på vilka sätt kan ett etnologiskt projekt påverka samhällets pandemiberedskap och pandemihantering? In: *Thule. Kungliga Skytteanska Samfundets Årsbok*.

Lundgren, Britta & Martin Holmberg 2015: Svininfluensapandemin i backspegeln. *Socialmedicinsk tidskrift* 92:6, 577–589.

Lundgren, Britta & Martin Holmberg 2017: Pandemic Flus and Vaccination Policies in Sweden. In: Christine Holmberg, Stuart Blume & Paul Greenough (eds.), *The Politics of Vaccination: A Global History*. Manchester: Manchester University Press.

MacPhail, Theresa 2010: A Predictable Unpredictability: The 2009 H1N1 Pandemic and the Concept of 'Strategic Uncertainty' within Global Public Health. *Behemoth: A Journal on Civilisation* 3, 57–77.

Martin, Emily 1994: *Flexible Bodies: The Role of Immunity in American Culture from the Days of Polio to the Age of AIDS*. Boston: Beacon Press.

MSB [Swedish Civil Contingencies Agency] & Socialstyrelsen [The National Board of Health and Welfare] 2011: Influensa A (H1N1) 2009 – utvärdering av förberedelser och hantering av pandemin. Stockholm, https://www.msb.se/upload/Nyheter_press/Influensa_A(H1N1)_2009.pdf?epslanguage=sv.

Neustadt, Richard E. & Harvey V. Fineberg 1978: *The Swine Flu Affair: Decision-Making on a Slippery Disease*. Washington DC: US Government Printing Office.

Nichter, Mark 2008: *Global Health: Why Cultural Perceptions, Social Representations, and Biopolitics Matter*. Tuscon: The University of Arizona Press.

Rabeharisoa, Vololona & Michel Callon 2004: Patients and Scientists in French Muscular Dystrophy Research. In: Sheila Jasanoff (ed.), *States of Knowledge: The Co-Production of Science and Social Order*. New York: Routledge.

Rabinow, Paul & Nicolas Rose 2006: Biopower Today. *BioSocieties* 1, 195–217.

Raman, Sujatha & Richard Tutton 2010: Life, Science, and Biopower. *Science Technology and Human Values* 35, 711–734.

Riessman, Catherine Kohler 2008: *Narrative Methods for the Human Sciences.* Thousand Oaks: SAGE Publishing.

Scoones, Ian 2010: Fighting the Flu: Risk, Uncertainty and Surveillance. In: Sarah Dry & Melissa Leach (eds.), *Epidemics: Science, Governance and Social Justice.* London: Earthscan.

Seljemaa, Elo-Hanna & Pihla Maria Siim 2016: Where Silence Takes us, if we Listen to it. *Ethnologia Europaea* 46:2, 5–13.

Singer, Merrill 2015: *Anthropology of Infectious Disease.* Walnut Creek: Left Coast Press.

Smittskyddsinstitutet 2011: Influenza A(H1N1) Pandemic in Sweden 2009–2010: A Report from the Swedish WHO National Influenza Centre, https://www.folkhalsomyndigheten.se/contentassets/1d7096c2b65d45b499c-924d76333272c/influenza-in-sweden-2009-2010.pdf.

Svenska Dagbladet 2009: Hemligt avtal styr vaccineringen. October 6, 2009.

Svenska Läkemedelsförsäkringen 2016: Pandemrix och narkolepsi. Update 13, July 21, 2016.

Trostle, James A. 2005: *Epidemiology and Culture.* Cambridge: Cambridge University Press.

Trundle, Catherine 2011: Biopolitical Endpoints: Diagnosing a Deserving British Nuclear Test Veteran. *Social Science & Medicine* 73, 882–888.

Trundle, Catherine & Brydie Isobel Scott 2013: Elusive Genes: Nuclear Test Veterans' Experiences of Genetic Citizenship and Biomedical Refusal. *Medical Anthropology* 32:6, 501–517, doi: 10.1080/01459740.2012.757606.

Vetenskapsrådet 2012: The Swedish Research Council's Mapping of Research Relevant to the Etiology and Treatment of the Disease Narcolepsy. Stockholm, Sweden.

Britta Lundgren is a professor of Ethnology at the Department of Culture and Media Studies, Umeå University, Sweden. Her research interests are medical humanities, pandemics and vaccination, and gender studies. One of her most recent publications is (together with Martin Holmberg): Pandemic Flus and Vaccination Policies in Sweden (in: C. Holmberg, S. Blume & P. Greenough, eds., *The Politics of Vaccination: A Global History*. Manchester: Manchester University Press).
(britta.lundgren@umu.se)

FLEXICURITY WITHOUT SECURITY
An Inquiry into the Danish Flexicurity Model in a Neoliberal Era

Niels Jul Nielsen, University of Copenhagen, and
Janus Jul Olsen, Chinese Academy of Sciences, Copenhagen Business School

The Danish flexicurity model is widely acknowledged and even advocated by the European Commission as a measure to achieve economic progress without compromising basic social conditions. It is therefore paradoxical that over the past decades the security component of the flexicurity model has faced steady retrenchments, jeopardizing its overall balance. The article applies a historical approach to understanding the transformation that has given way to a weakened position of workers in society, and asserts that the changes of the flexicurity model have been conditioned by the disappearance of the view of the "working class" as a potential threat to societal peace – a change closely connected to the waning of an alternative to capitalism and the related opportunity for a spread of neoliberal political economy.

Keywords: flexicurity, neoliberalism, Keynesianism, Cold War, deregulation

The Danish Flexicurity Model

The Danish flexicurity model is generally regarded as a central component of Denmark's welfare regime. Through liberal dismissal regulations, high unemployment benefits and active labour market policies, a mobile and well-functioning labour market system has been institutionalized as an integral part of the Danish welfare state, benefitting both social partners (Andersen & Mailand 2005; Bredgaard & Kongshøj Madsen 2015; Jensen 2017; Kongshøj Madsen 2008). In its basic definition, the flexicurity model is the institutional system that on the one hand allows employers to easily hire and fire, and on the other hand guarantees employees financial security through high unemployment benefits and higher probability of re-employment; employers do not fear difficulties or high costs related to firing employees. While these two components are considered to be the main axes of the Danish flexicurity model, the model possesses a third component: active labour market policies. These serve to redirect the unemployed into the labour market, increasing the likelihood of re-employment (Kongshøj Madsen 2008). Flexicurity thus manages to navigate between a capitalist market economy and a demand for social justice and safety:

> The fundamental idea behind the concept of flexicurity is that flexibility and security are not contradictory to one another, but in many situations can be mutually supportive. Furthermore, flexibility is not the monopoly of the employers,

just as security is not the monopoly of the employees. [...] So, the foundation is there for a new interaction between flexibility and security, which stresses the potential for win-win outcomes in situations, which are traditionally conceived as characterised by conflicting interests. (Kongshøj Madsen 2008: 3)

The security component of the Danish flexicurity model, with an increased focus on minimizing the deficits of unemployment, was built from the beginning of the twentieth century and especially prioritized in the post-war welfare regime. The model is closely related to the structure of the so-called Danish Model, characterized by (relatively) independently acting social partners that act through mutual recognition (Due & Madsen 1993; Due, Madsen & Jensen 1993; Jensen 2015). In 1899, the labour unions and the employers' organisations agreed on the so-called September Compromise, as the Danish workers accepted employers' right to liberally hire and fire employees. In return, workers were allowed to organize and were acknowledged as a collective actor with the mandate to negotiate wages and work conditions that were settled through collective agreements (Ibsen & Jørgensen 1978; Jensen 2015; Jul Nielsen 2002). The Danish Model thus can be seen as a dynamic institutional arrangement, which constitutes the Danish industrial relations system, as the model is built on negotiation between social partners to reach collective agreements.[1] An important characteristic of the Danish Model has been that the percentage of organized workers has been large, and this has provided the system with a high level of legitimacy. However, similar to what can be observed across Europe (Strøby Jensen 2004), weakened Danish unions have experienced slowly declining membership rates, from 73 percent in 1995 to 67 percent in 2010; if the membership of the increasingly successful yellow unions (comparable to mere insurance agencies and not involved in agreement negotiations) is deducted, the decline in the same period is from 71 percent to 61 percent (Due, Pihl & Madsen 2010: 19). Although memberships are still relatively high compared to other countries, the prospect of a continuous decline points to a loss of critical mass that will eventually jeopardize the legitimacy of the trade unions as a basic pillar of labour market regulation.

Flexicurity and the EU

Flexicurity has won international recognition because it combines market efficiency with social concerns.[2] Though flexicurity can take many forms,[3] it was the Danish version of it that the EU Commission regarded as the ideal when it adopted flexicurity as a key concept within the European Employment strategy in 2006–2007 (Jensen 2017), as "a crucial element in modernising the EU's labour market" (Eur-Lex 2007a). The following excerpt reveals the reason behind the acknowledgment of the Danish flexicurity model:

> The Danish labour market shows a successful combination of flexibility and security, offering flexible labour laws and relatively low job protection, extensive efforts on lifelong learning and active labour market policies, and a generous social security system. (Eur-Lex 2007b)

By 2006, the European Commission had adopted the concept of flexicurity, regarding it to be an instrumental element in EU's goal to create both social cohesion and a competitive labour market. As José Manuel Barroso stated in 2006 at the Year of Workers' Mobility Launch Conference, "This concept of 'flexicurity' is a way of ensuring that employers and workers feel they have the flexibility, but also the security they need" (Keune & Jepsen 2007: 8).

Flexicurity is thus regarded by the European Union as a model that makes it possible to maintain popular support for liberal dismissal policies. And as the following excerpt shows, Denmark is regarded as a prime example of how flexicurity can be carried out successfully:

> The Dutch and Danish experience are interpreted as proof that alternative approaches to simple deregulation can be successful in providing high levels of flexibility, without this being at the cost

of increased workers' insecurity. Hence, flexicurity would offer options for a market with a human face, fitting European varieties of capitalism better than the deregulation approach which dominates American capitalism. (Keune & Jepsen 2007: 6)

Given the widespread acknowledgement of the Danish flexicurity model, it stands out as a paradox that the security component of it has come increasingly under strain (Andersen, Mailand & Ibsen 2012; Jul Nielsen 2004; Jørgensen 2011; Kongshøj Madsen 2011).[4] In the following sections, we will examine the underlying historical transformations that we argue are pivotal to understanding such a development as more than merely a superficial outcome of economic fluctuations (culminating with the financial crisis in 2008). First, we turn to a brief historical account of the development in unemployment benefits as one of the basic security components of the Danish flexicurity model. We do not intend to make a comprehensive analysis of the entire security dimension of flexicurity in the Danish context, which would entail a detailed account of the spectrum of active labour market policies and the relationship between these policies and unemployment benefits (where development of the former in line with neoliberal reasoning could be advocated to partially replace the withdrawal of the latter). Rather, our aim is to illustrate how the historical development of unemployment benefits illuminates a shift in the approach to social welfare.

Theoretical and Methodological Foundation

As a basis for our argumentation throughout the article, we will briefly present key components of its applied theoretical framework, as gazing through this lens enables an understanding of the underlying foundation for the further analysis of the macropolitical transitions that have resulted in the changing conditions for the Danish flexicurity model.

The theoretical lens that this article applies is the ethnological state and life-mode theory, which parallels neo-Marxist scholarship and is aligned with social scientists and ethnologists such as Boserup (1986), Højrup (2003), Kaspersen (2012), and Kaspersen and Gabriel (2005). Through different terminologies these scholars perceive the state as a subject, and the social groups within the states as life-modes (Højrup's terminology, see later) that are understood as dependent subjects whose conditions of existence rely on state recognition. The approach applies the German philosopher G.W.F. Hegel's concept of *recognition* to explain how a relation of mutual recognition between states determines the state's external position. A state must be strong enough to be recognized by the other states in the state-system. This strength is rooted internally in the individual state: in the army, the civil society, the economy, the institutional systems etc. The state's struggle for recognition in the state-system is therefore closely connected to the internal landscape of the state, this implying that the dependent subjects' conditions of existence are realized on the state's premises, serving as a means to the state's survival (for a detailed account of this way of employing a Hegelian inspired conceptual hierarchy, see Højrup 2003). Obviously, social practices are not necessarily initiated "from above"; but if they jeopardize the principal concerns of the state, they will not endure, or the state will collapse. The rise of a conscious labour population in the late nineteenth century is an example of a movement "from below", which, following resistance from the state, was split in a complex process into a politically recognized part (evolving into labour unions, political parties and other organisations) and non-recognized factions (radical anti-system organisations and groups) that were regarded as destabilizing to the state (Jul Nielsen 2002).

To understand how the external struggle for recognition is related to the way in which workers as a social group have been handled within the Danish state in different periods, this article applies a methodology of historical analysis. Hereby it is illuminated how developments in the external milieu of the Danish state have conditioned different internal perceptions and priorities of social groups against the background of larger political and economic transformations. In the ethnological endeavour to understand the principal relation between ways of living and the conditions on which these are based, a historical analysis can illuminate how and why basic living conditions for particular life-modes undergo a transformation.

Unemployment Benefits under Strain

Danish unemployment benefits have suffered severe retrenchments over the past decades. Unemployment benefits peaked in the mid-1970s and have since then declined gradually (Mailand 2010). In essence, the Danish unemployment benefits are constituted by three components: (1) the degree to which the benefits cover the original wage of the unemployed; (2) the amount of time during which the unemployed is entitled to receive benefits; (3) the temporal requirements for accruing the right to receive unemployment benefits. Since the early 1980s, all three have been drastically cut back. An analysis made in 2004 by the Danish Confederation of Trade Unions (LO) showed that compensations since 1982 had been reduced by 25 percent. With the labour market reform in 1993–94, the period in which one could receive unemployment benefits was fixed at seven years, from a previously de facto unlimited time period, while continuous retrenchments followed until 1999 when it was fixed at four years. In the 1990s, the opposition and the unions accepted these reductions in unemployment benefit period because they received extended active labour market initiatives in return. For instance in 1996, when the unemployment benefit period was reduced to five years, full time activation was imposed after two years of unemployment (Mailand 2010: 6).

The financial crisis in 2008 took its toll on the Danish economy, as it did across Europe. From an unemployment rate close to structural unemployment (3.4 percent) prior to the crisis, the unemployment rate was doubled in 2010. With the unemployment benefit reform (*Dagpengereformen*) in 2010, severe amendments were made to the Danish unemployment benefits. The period of receiving benefits was halved from four to two years, while the accruing requirement (*genoptjeningskravet*) was doubled: the work requirement went from 26 weeks within three years to at least 52 weeks within three years (Mailand 2015). Although the continuous retrenchments have caused public debate and political controversies in the left and right, the downward tendency has been almost independent of the political leanings of the government in power. Thus, when a centre-left government took over in 2011, it restricted itself to implementing acute and temporary policies to ease the immediate negative effects from a recent reform made by the previous administration, rather than policies with the overall aim of reversing reductions from previous years. In other words, the established view across political parties (with the exception of those to the far political left) has been to use flexibility to meet market demands, pushing security concerns to the side-line.

What we argue – by examining unemployment benefits – is that an aggravation of the security component of the flexicurity model does not stand alone as evidence of a weakened labour side. It is closely connected with a decline in influence of the Danish trade unions (the background of which we will return to). Several concrete political initiatives since the millennium have had direct influence on the unions' conditions. In 2002, the Danish government, for instance, implemented an act that dissolved the bonds between a particular unemployment fund and a particular trade union, allowing for the yellow unions to flourish (Kjellberg & Ibsen 2016). In 2006, in addition, it implemented an act that abolished the right to let employment be conditioned by membership in a particular trade union. These initiatives among others have resulted in declines in membership from the red unions; and even during the latest social democratic government, the relationship to the unions was close to the breaking point (Jensen 2017).

It is relevant to include another example of how the general framework of worker protection has undergone a transition. The European open border system – embedded in the Schengen agreement and the tenets of the four freedoms (freedom of capital, commodities, services and labour) – has brought about an increased competition that severely impacts worker livelihoods. With the addition of ten new countries during the EU enlargement in 2004 (including eight from the former Eastern bloc), workers from low-wage and high-wage countries became part of the same labour market. The open border system provided the former with new opportunities abroad, while the latter were subjected to competition of a kind that had been avoided for decades due to influential labour organisations. As Randall Hansen – focusing on West Germany, Great Britain and France but arguing it to be a pattern applying also to other Northern European countries – has illustrated: when the first afterwar waves of labour migration were seen in the 1960s, strong labour unions in the receiving countries had the power to safeguard that the guest-workers were granted wage and working conditions equal to the domestic workers, that they were generally integrated in the unionized system, and that they managed to curb the influx to limited quotas (Hansen 2003). That labour migration since the 1990s has managed to stress job security, wages and working conditions (Andreß & Lohmann 2008; Favell 2008, 2009; Friberg 2012; Jul Nielsen & Sandberg 2014; Lubanski 1999; Stan & Erne 2016; Standing 2011) reveals a much weaker and less influential labour agenda that has lost the political support it had half a century ago. In Denmark since 2004, the number of so-called Eastern workers (from the former Eastern bloc countries) has continued to rise, thereby challenging conditions within sectors with low-skilled jobs such as construction, cleaning and agriculture (Andersen & Felbo-Kolding 2013; Andersen & Pedersen 2007; Bræmer & Redder 2017; Jul Nielsen 2016; Andersen & Arnholz 2007).

Thus, we argue that the changes witnessed during the previous decades in the Danish flexicurity model are symptoms of a principal transformation of the recognition of workers as a particular societal group, and not merely of shifting currents of political orientation. In the following section, we examine two macropolitical changes that have taken place during the twentieth century, which, we argue, can be understood as catalysts for the retrenchments that have been imposed on the security component of the Danish flexicurity model since the 1980s. Although we mainly focus on Danish material here, and specifically on the Danish flexicurity model, we see these transformations as evidence of an overall decline of labour influence that has taken place not only in Denmark but also across Europe (Andreß & Lohmann 2008; Standing 2011; Strøby Jensen 2004).

Bringing in a Historical Perspective on the Political Economy and Theorizing "Class"

The first systemic change has been a paradigmatic shift from a Keynesian to a neoliberal paradigm in the political economy, beginning with the Thatcher era in the late 1970s. The term neoliberalism is ambiguous; in some cases it refers narrowly to a macroeconomic doctrine, while in others it is used as a broad reference to capitalism and global inequalities. In the present article we see it as a form of political economy that favours deregulation, free trade, privatization and other regulatory forms that are based on market logic, which implies that a market is not understood as a pre-social form but rather as a political creation (Harvey 2005; Wacquant 2012: 71). Accordingly, just like politics matter in a neoliberal regime, liberal currents played an important role during the era of (what could generally be referred to as) Keynesianism. This era also embraced a diversity of specific regimes, ranging for example from the social democratic systems of Scandinavia with (relatively) independently acting social partners to more corporatist models of continental Europe. Despite the variety of forms, neoliberalism emerged as the anti-thesis to the Keynesian regimes, highlighting the idea of the free possessive individual as a contrast to state-led social engineering (S. Hall 2011: 706). We will later return to what could be argued to be a paradigmatic shift to a neoliberal political economy during the 1970s and 1980s. For the moment, it is relevant to reiterate that this shift, along with a general pressure on the European welfare states from an increasingly globalized economy, has given rise, since the 1980s, to a slow but steady challenge to the voice of labour. Through the discursive agenda set by a neoliberal paradigm, it is generally perceived as less and less legitimate, both economically and socially, to provide social security on a collective basis.

Another principal macropolitical change – and arguably also an important condition for the spread of neoliberalism – during the previous half century has been the gradual diminishing of the "working class" as a potential political threat. Without engaging in a lengthy exposé concerning the concept of the "working class"[5], it is nevertheless appropriate to relate the theoretical framework employed in the present article to the way in which the notion of "class" has played a role in both academia and the public discourse. State and life-mode theory that has been developed since the 1980s is rooted in a Marxian framework (Højrup 2003). The concept of *mode of production* and thus people's distinct relation to "processes of production and the disposition of the product" (Carrier 2015: 29) are regarded as key to an understanding of reproducible ways of living: *life-modes*. Notably, unlike many Marxist usages of the notion of class, a life-mode should not be regarded as an empirical category of human beings, but as a concept that designates principally different ways of upholding a viable existence (Marx himself was ambiguous on this point and never finished the last chapter of *Capital*, in which he begins to elaborate what it is that constitutes "class"). The theoretically determined life-mode concepts themselves make up necessary preconditions for the reproduction of the (theoretically determined) *modes of production* that are regarded as necessary in a given social formation. The concept of the *capitalist mode of production*, for instance, requires three (concepts of) life-modes for its reproduction: an investor life-mode (providing necessary production apparatus and working capital) and two life-modes that contribute to different forms of "work", principally distinct from each other. The *wage-earner* life-mode provides work of a predefined kind (requiring more or less skill) and the *career-professional* life-mode contributes undefined ideas and skills that provide a company with the necessary innovative edge to put it ahead of competitors, which is key to the survival of the company.

In general, it can be argued that since the 1980s, systemic understandings have fallen victim to an increasing interest in agency, "culminating in the emergence of postmodernism which often became a rejection of all systems" (Carrier 2015: 37) This scholarly development dissolved the view of a concept such as class, as having relevant analytical bearing; and, notably not only when concerned with contemporary circumstances. As historian Gareth Stedmann Jones phrased it in 1983, "'class' is a discursive rather than (...) an ontological reality" (Stedman Jones 1983: 7). Historian Patrick Joyce furthered this idea, concluding from an analysis of nineteenth-century material that, "Other forms of the self and of collective identity emerge, long obscured by the concentration on class" (Joyce 1994). In general, "class" became disregarded as a primary concept for understanding everyday culture, in favour of concepts such as "identity" that are supposedly more sensitive to empirical complexity (Carrier, Kalb & Carbonella 2015: 19; Jul Nielsen 2013b, 2016). To the extent that the concept of class was regarded as a token of a shared, homogenous worker's culture, postmodernism's critique was correct and timely; the self and the social take many forms, and relevant are also issues of gender, race and nationalism (Berlanstein 1993; Boris & Janssens 1999; Boyd & McWilliam 1995; Carrier 2015), patterns of attitudes (Ambjörnsson 1988; Horgby 1993; Lüdtke 1986), and many other forms of "the social". However, postmodernism does not provide a possible hierarchy of the infinite aspects that influence culture; as Carrier provocatively puts it (while advocating a renewed focus on class and systemic understandings), "the drift in anthropology since the 1970s has been toward description without analysis… we can begin to ask, once more, not just questions about what and how, but also questions about why and where it leads" (Carrier 2015: 39f.)

The concept of life-mode includes a multitude of relations and social identifications; but with the theory's focus on cultural practices' ability to reproduce themselves (and thus a matter of principal importance for this article), the basic conditions for the continuance of a life-mode has precedence over other aspects of the practice. In the case of a wage-earner life-mode, a theoretical need to create *wage-earner monopolies* can be determined. A person who lives from the sale of predefined tasks of some sort will always be exposed to underselling (since such tasks have an abundant supply of labour). Consequently, it is necessary to find a way to monopolize the supply of work to prevent an open competition in the commodity of labour. Monopolization can take the form of organized unions, but it can also rely on informal relations such as groups of workers engaging in a personal relationship with an employer. Monopolization can imply an *avoidance* of union organization in order to bring together an attractive group of cheap labour, as can be observed in some cases with migrant workers (Jul Nielsen 2013b, 2016; Jul Nielsen & Sandberg 2014). Moreover, wage-earner monopolies are always in a mutual competitive relation to each other (for an elaboration of the concept of wage-earner monopolies, the necessary co-existence of inclusion and exclusion that it implies, and the connection to the writings of Marx, see Jul Nielsen 2002, 2013a). Thus, no matter the form in which we find groups of workers – gendered, nationalistic, diligent, rebellious, etc. – we must be able to account for the way in which this cultural pattern does not contradict the basic demand to maintain a livelihood that is conditioned by some sort of wage-earner monopoly. Later, we briefly return to how state- and life-mode theory not only operates on the level of life-modes and modes of production, but – in contrast to a Marxian legacy – puts precedence on the concept of the state; the state is understood as ultimately conditioning the life-modes and thus also the practice as a worker.

The scholarly discussions of what constitutes the working class as a theoretical concept have regularly been entangled in the societal discourse, where the use of the notion served to attain influence for left-wingers, both with and without working-class roots. The term "labour", on the other hand, was often used to refer more broadly to ordinary people or "the common man". The "working class" in the public discourse is largely a notion that refers to the world order that existed prior to the collapse of the Soviet Union, and it has disappeared with the decline of workers' discursive influence; symptomatically, the notion is regaining usage following Brexit and the election of Trump for president, incidents that have recreated a political focus on workers.

When bringing in a historical approach it leaps to the eye how "labour", throughout most of the twentieth century, and notably in the Keynesian era, generally represented a top priority on the political agenda. But since the 1980s, labour organisations and unions (which moreover as mentioned have a declining membership) have generally found themselves in a weaker bargaining position when negotiating terms and conditions with the employers' organisations, as governments (leaning on neoliberal ideology) have become less inclined to support union demands. The weak position of "labour" is closely linked with the aforementioned prevalence of a neoliberal policy paradigm, and we argue below that neoliberalism's triumphal progress is only understandable alongside the significant transformations in the state system. The collapse of the Soviet Union and the end of the Cold War constituted – at least for a period – a de facto end to an alternative to capitalism, as the formerly planned economies were integrated into the world economy. With these changes, the image of the "working class" as a potential threat vanished. Although for decades a revolutionary prospect had been rather unlikely (despite continuous radical rhetoric well into the 1980s), the transition, as we argue below, gradually caused a decline in the influence of "labour".

Most of the literature on Danish flexicurity revolves around the model itself. It deals with its historical development, specific elements, latest changes, or contemporary opinions on flexicurity (Andersen & Hansen 2007; Bredgaard & Kongshøj Madsen 2015; Jensen 2015; Keune & Jepsen 2007; Mailand 2010, 2015). While these approaches are obviously important to understand the model and its role in determining working conditions, they do not comprehend the preconditions of the model in a broader perspective. To grasp the extent of the changes of how flexicurity is realized, it is relevant to inquire into the transformation of the role of "labour" in a political and ideological context. This is not limited to Denmark but applies in general terms to Western Europe, although specific forms of welfare politics and of labour market and social organisation vary across the European states. Through such a lens, we may be equipped with an analytical tool capable of explaining, in macropolitical terms, why the model has gone through the development it has, allowing for a qualified conjecture about future prospects.

Labour's Role in the Post-War Period

Why is it that "labour" played such a prominent role on the social agenda from the end of the nineteenth century and well into the 1980s? The common answer to this revolves around the industrialization of European societies in the second half of the nineteenth century that brought about the establishment of a new class – the "working class" – forced to sell its labour in order to create a sustainable livelihood. By organizing collectively, it succeeded in putting pressure on employers; and as a result, gradually "from below" managed to raise wage and working conditions. Though this perspective is not incorrect, we argue that to fully understand the rise and fall of labour influence during the subsequent more than 150 years, it is necessary to include the role of the states in which the social partners act. Thus, as already touched upon, labour influence is not only a matter of a movement "from below", but also – and maybe ultimately conditioned by – recognition "from above".

As stated previously, our theoretical argument is based on the deduction that for a state to hold sufficient strength for recognition *externally* in the state system, there must be an *internal* endeavour to create sufficient cohesion and legitimacy. Thus, the lifemodes (as well as modes of production) that achieve the necessary recognition that conditions their endurance, such as workers' right to organize and act collectively, are the life-modes that are pivotal for the viability of the state. In line with this, we argue that states' struggle for survival in the state system impacts national contexts, including the way in which social partners are understood and acknowledged, and thus also the relative strength of each partner. This theoretical reasoning provides the analysis with a conceptual hierarchy: no life-mode or mode of production can endure without the recognition of the state that ultimately conditions it, whereas a state does not necessarily need its life-modes and modes of production to survive.

To substantiate the argument empirically, we include below an example that unambiguously displays how "labour" previously held a key political role which is principally different from what we find today. The example is explored extensively in the book *Between High Politics and the Workshop Floor: The Danish Worker – Before, During and After the Cold War* (Jul Nielsen 2004; see also Jul Nielsen 2014), where the role of "labour" is examined in relation to the strategic concerns of the state from the end of the nineteenth century until today by looking at Danish history. The example epitomizes in a clear-cut way how the political recognition of and influence given to one social group – in this case workers – is connected to overall defence and security concerns of the state; a connection that will often be of a more indirect kind and thus more difficult to apprehend.

The case in point dates back to 1953, at the height of the Cold War, with a NATO conference held in Copenhagen. Representatives of the political establishment were present from all member states: Canada, France, Great Britain, Belgium, Luxembourg, Italy, Greece, Portugal, Turkey, Iceland, Norway, and Denmark – along with the United States, the undisputed hegemon of the alliance. The objective of the conference reveals unmistakably how security matters concerned not only military power:

> NATO [should make up] an efficient manifestation of the unity of the member states in not only military but also, and equally importantly, in non-military matters, which touch upon political, economic and social problems within the countries. In the long run, a military defence in itself is not sufficient to guard the grounding of Western democracy.[6]

In the mid-1950s, the Cold War was at its height, and with both a militarily, politically and ideologically strong Soviet Union, the West, with the United States as the frontrunner, needed much more than mere military power to withstand the Eastern threat. In the early post-war years, despite criticisms, communism and socialism as alternatives to capitalism appealed to millions of people in the West, not least among the working class. There was the risk that radical sentiments amongst the populace could turn against the established order. Social cohesion within civil society was pivotal for the strength of the Western societies; and the radicalism of the 1930s stood as a fresh and frightening memory. It is in this context that "labour" assumed a top priority on the political agenda, a situation that seems highly foreign to international politics since the 1990s. The conference – concerned with youth politics, housing, education and a wide range of other topics connected to civil society – plainly concluded that integration of "labour" was the primary concern, with other issues being pushed to the side. In straightforward words – characteristically with the American spelling of "labor", this reflecting USA's stamp on the conference (where statements and declarations had been prepared in advance) – the principal statement of the conference was: "The role of labor in world affairs has become a key factor."

The reasoning behind this unambiguous statement was that "labour" was the target of propaganda from the East, and it was among the working populations that rebellious opinions could gain a stronger foothold. Therefore, it is no surprise that the conference concluded that labour organizations and labour parties should be provided with profound potential to influence society to improve workers' livelihoods. This was regarded as a means to dismantle the critiques of Western capitalism and its alleged suppression of the "little man". Labour representatives were given a voice in order to allow for "more effective attention to the problems of workers' standards of living such as purchasing power, employment, housing needs… etc.". As we return to below, this strategy paralleled in economic terms the priority that Keynesianism – the preferred economic tool of the period – put on maintaining a high level of employment (with the social unrest of the 1930s as contrasting scenario) as well as general attention to workers' demands.[7]

Thus, the statements from the 1953 NATO conference explicitly reveals how the inclusion of "labour" as a basic pillar in the running of society is dependent upon the particular security focus of the state (or in this case a coalition of states merged together by the Eastern counterpart). As said, we are well aware that similar unambiguous statements cannot necessarily be found in the source material in other periods. However, we argue that the accentuated circumstances of the conference reveal a logic that has been dominant for over a century, from socialism's emergence as a potential political threat in the second half of the nineteenth century until the end of the twentieth century (see Jul Nielsen 2004, 2013a). To illustrate this, we will present from two other transitory periods, two examples that reveal a similar pattern:

Across Europe the Paris Commune of 1871 left no room for doubt among the political establishment that a socialist (or communist) revolt had to be regarded as a potential threat. As a result, labour assemblies and actions were increasingly perceived in this light (Bruun 1938; Jul Nielsen 2002). As is well known, the labour movement was gravely divided on the question of either a radical revolutionary upheaval of capitalist society or a more graduate reformism (with the ultimate goal of socialism pushed to an undefined future). In general, the European states gradually, at the expense of the radicals, recognized the moderate wings of the labour movement that became increasingly influential. As Richard Hyman writes, "Trade unions… varied between (and often within) countries; but typically, the latter half of the nineteenth century saw the more successful unions marginalizing or ritualizing their radicalism, and seeking understandings with employers on the basis of a 'fair day's wage for a fair day's work'" (Hyman 2001: 2).

The years following the First World War were again marked by mass mobilization among Europe's working populations. The Bolshevik Revolution in 1917 and subsequent establishment of communist parties across Europe (and in the U.S., sparking off an intense Red Scare [Levin 1971; Schmidt 2000]) underlined the distinction between the moderate and the anti-system wing of the labour movement, providing the former with convincing arguments for improved worker welfare in order to dismantle the latter. Thus, the 1920s and 1930s throughout Europe saw an extension of broad social programs in housing, education, sickness insurance, old age provision, etc., similar to what came to mark the post-World War Two welfare states. The 1953 NATO conference epitomized this shift.

It is important to note that in most European countries the threat of a communist or socialist takeover was probably never a real possibility; and indeed, there was not broad support for communism after the invasion of Hungary in 1956. Still, a threat of mass mobilisation around socialist ideology was an efficient *means* for "labour" to maintain the significant influence. The 1960s and 1970s, despite the weakening of communism, were heavily marked by radical and revolutionary rhetoric, with persistent references to the interests of the "working class" (although often originating in the middle class) that maintained the political influence. It was not until the collapse of the Eastern bloc that an alternative to capitalism ultimately disappeared and entirely removed the threat potential and the possibility of using this to achieve bargaining power and influence. Inner political and ideological cohesion of the state as a precondition for external strength no longer relied on "labour" as a defined social group.

From Keynesianism to Neoliberalism

The shift in the power balance within the state system – culminating in the fall of the Soviet empire – was also pivotal to the spread of neoliberalism as the other major transformation that comprised a principal challenge to "labour". The emergence of a neoliberal policy paradigm in the West in the late 1970s contributed to a continuous weakening of the "working class" and thus also a weakening of the powers (unions and leftist parties) that advocated a strong social security net and worker welfare (Baglioni & Crouch 1990; Crouch 2013; P.A. Hall 1993; Rodgers 2011; Streeck 2006).

The analysis of the English path to neoliberalism by political economist Peter A. Hall illuminates the processes that other European countries also underwent. Hall enquires into the general steps whereby policies change and analyses how a new policy paradigm emerged in Britain in the late 1970s with Margaret Thatcher coming to power. Parallel to Kuhn's thinking on scientific paradigms (Kuhn 1962), Hall describes how a policy paradigm is embedded in the terminology used to communicate it. Just as a scientific paradigm is institutionalized in the language that reproduces it, a policy paradigm is reproduced through the institutions that constitute it. It is not until a sufficient amount of anomalies occur that it becomes possible to critically analyse the paradigm itself. Before that, any criticisms will be targeted towards constitutions *within* the scientific paradigm, not its foundation. Hall describes this in regards to policymaking, illuminating the difference between what he terms first, second, and third order changes. First and second order are changes that "adjust policy without challenging the overall terms of a given policy paradigm, much like 'normal science'". In contrast, third order changes are "marked by radical changes in the overarching terms of policy discourse associated with a 'paradigm-shift'" (Hall 1993: 281ff.).

Hall argues that the former Keynesian policy paradigm fell victim to a third order change. In the post-war period, Keynes' coherent system of ideas was institutionalised and applied within the financial systems around Europe, "They became the prism through which policymakers saw the economy as well as their own role within it" (ibid.: 283ff.). However, this economic order did not, as we know, sustain itself in the long run. Hall mentions three implications that will be present when policy paradigm changes occur. The first is scientific opposition to the existing paradigm, which to some extent must also manifest itself politically. Second, Hall points to the significance of authoritative figures who actually will have the vision and power to advocate for and begin the process of implementing the set of new political and economic ideas. The third implication is the accumulation of anomalies within the old paradigm, which have been dealt with unsuccessfully through the methods prevalent in the old paradigm.

All three conditions were present during the 1970s when neoliberalism first entered the scene in Britain. Anomalies – for example the simultaneous increase in both unemployment and inflation that should not be possible – had accumulated during the past decades. Such anomalies were unsuccessfully dealt with through ad hoc-attempts of changing, for instance, the fiscal policies, resulting in an extended distrust of the system and paving the way for an alternative path (ibid.: 285). In 1974, the neoliberalists Friedrich von Hayek and Milton Friedman shared the Nobel Prize in Economics; and with such alternative perceptions of the economy gaining a footing, the strong, authoritative figure of Margaret Thatcher represented a viable alternative to Keynesianism when she was elected in 1979. This evolved into a fundamental fight against the labour side during the 1980s, which would have been virtually unimaginable a few decades earlier when attention to workers' demands was the top political priority as a precaution against societal disintegration. Notably, similar occurrences took place in other European countries, although typically a few years later and in a less radical form.

With neoliberalism comes a whole new set of goals and policy instruments that shift the political landscape. Several of these instruments directly impact conditions pivotal for workers' livelihood:

> Inflation replaced unemployment as the preeminent concern of policymakers. Macroeconomic efforts to reduce unemployment were rejected in favour of balanced budgets and direct tax reductions. Monetary policy replaced fiscal policy as the principal macroeconomic instrument, and it was reoriented towards fixed targets for the rate of monetary growth. Many regulatory instruments associated with state intervention, such as incomes policies, exchange controls, and quantitative limits on bank lending, were eliminated. (Hall 1993)

Neoliberal ideology does not perceive the prosperity of the "working class" as a goal or as a means. Instead, it is the belief that the market forces, with little or no state intervention, bring balance into the economy and thus create the strongest and most resistant society. As Colin Crouch puts it, "neoliberals [are]… unequivocally hostile to trade unions, which seek to interfere with the smooth operation of the labour market" (Crouch 2013: 18). In contrast to the Keynesian paradigm, in a neoliberal society the state does not have any ideological or instrumental incentives to support labour organisations, as they are perceived as obstacles to the flourishing of market forces.

It is relevant also to point to the disappearance of traditional industrial workplaces in Western Europe to explain declining labour influence and the lack of identification with "the working class". Overall, during the 1970s and 1980s, the Western industrialized countries lost their monopoly on global surplus-extraction. Fordist production processes became the source of revenues in non-Western countries, most notably in the Asian tiger economies, and this pushed the Western economies to improve knowledge-content within production to maintain a competitive edge, thus safeguarding an adequate individual profit margin in the market. The subsequent increasing fluidity of capital and spread of liberal trading agreements (advocated by international organisations such as the WTO, established in 1995) has increased the pace of out-sourcing, off-shoring or closures, forcing a reconfiguration of the working population (Hochschild 2016; Højrup 2017; Jul Nielsen 2004; LiPuma & Lee 2004; Sennett 1998, 2006; Standing 2009). These economic transitions are important for the influence of labour but should not be seen as independently working "factors".

First, the presence of "classic" workplaces is not a purely economic matter. During the Keynesian era such workplaces were extensively supported by the states – well-known examples are shipyards and the mining industry. This state support was due to an inclination towards economic protectionism as well as the fear of the social unrest that would result if such companies were to close down in the face of pure market forces. Without digging into the causes or probable broader consequences of president Trump's remarkable revitalization of a protectionist approach, this situation illuminates how economy is not developing per abstract laws but is politically conditioned. Further, one could argue that in a way Trump has merely adopted measures (and explicitly aimed to give renewed influence to the working population) that were widespread until the 1980s, when they were neglected in the neoliberal political economy, not least (and indeed paradoxically) due to American pressure to internationalize and liberalize markets.

Second, as specified above, what principally characterizes a wageworker job is not that it is manual and takes place at companies with many people; it is that the content of the job is predefined (whether requiring more or less skill). This is what marks the borderline to "knowledge work", where the basic requirement is that the employee contributes undefined ideas and skills that provide the company with an innovative edge that competitors do not possess. Predefined jobs will always be challenged by underpricing if they are not protected (for example by the monopolization of them that unions safeguard). And, notably, such jobs are not disappearing. They are found in large quantities throughout the labour market: in retail, service, production, agriculture, construction, cleaning, health, etc. If wage and working conditions in such occupations are left to market forces, a downward spiral is unavoidable; just like the Danish flexicurity model's security dimension will further diminish if not prioritized politically – without proper political supports only flexibility will be left, ultimately leading to social dumping.

Danish Flexicurity in the New World Order

Thus, a principal transformation has taken place from an overall Keynesian paradigm during the Cold War period to the present neoliberal era. During the Cold War period, "labour" played a key role as a precondition for social cohesion within the Western world. As a consequence, workers' organizations had a substantial influence on state affairs, which made union support a natural choice of the individual labourer. Following the collapse of the Eastern Bloc, neoliberal ideology and governance has succeeded in setting a new agenda. As a consequence, the prevalent view since the 1990s has increasingly been that market concerns are the natural nexus around which labour relations should revolve, making a political support for worker welfare appear to be an artificial inference with mechanisms of the market.

This transformation is crucial for the balance of the Danish flexibility model. With a continuous weakening of the unions, and with the Danish left-wing parties (in particular the Social Democratic party) moving towards the right, there are fewer forces that oppose neoliberal initiatives.[8] This process has revealed how a balanced flexicurity model depends on strong labour representation; and that such a state of affairs requires significant political support. Denmark's industrial relations have, as mentioned, been built upon negotiations between the "independent" social partners, with the government on the side-line. And not only have the Danish unions traditionally been strong, with high membership; but the state has also traditionally backed up the unions in the negotiations, rather than the employers, for reasons discussed previously.

Not surprisingly considering the transformations in the role of "labour", this arrangement is also changing. Trade unionists, who have worked for years in the labour movement, point to a shift in the political inclination to support the worker agenda over the employer agenda. In the excerpt below, a Danish union chairman, who has had a long trajectory as shipyard worker and shop-steward, followed by a career within the labour organisation, sums up the way in which the role of state, as one of the "legs" in the Danish model, has undergone a transition. The interview was conducted in 2011 in connection to an inquiry concerning the challenges involved in maintaining working conditions despite the increased influx of migrant workers from Eastern Europe to Denmark. However, the union chairman more generally reflects on the transformation of bargaining power despite the continued adherence to the Danish model of tripartite negotiations.

> Even though there will be many in the labour movement that will not like what I say now, actually, the most important system [around the Danish model] is not the unions, it is the political system! It all depends on having a government

and a state that want to play the game; because, all the same, the state has the power to play the game with other cards, in case it should be necessary. Thus, the weakest leg in the Danish system has been the employers. The employer side has adapted, but has not been especially active. We have historically seen a correlation between the trade-union movement and, typically, a Social Democratic government… well, also right-wing governments… that has built up the Danish model. Those are the two legs that need to interplay: the trade-union movement and the political level; if they manage to do that, then the employers will adapt automatically. However, if there is no recognition of this anymore, and much point in that direction… well, that is the deathblow to the Danish model.

The reasoning of the trade unionist illustrates how a particular consensus has been prevalent within the Danish model. The government in power – left-wing as well as right-wing – has generally been in support of the unions, arguably, we could add, as a result of the shared consensus about preventing "labour" from turning against the social order. Since the end of the 1980s, however, with the spread of neoliberal ideology, the legitimacy of the (red) trade unions has increasingly been questioned; and the monopolistic features of the unionized system have been found to be too restrictive for a sound economy.

The unions' legitimacy as the institutions that represent workers has thus suffered a hard blow; and it is disclosed that their former strength relied on political support "from above". That they are treated today as an obstacle to a smoothly running economy is not the result of new political insight but rather of the disappearance of "labour" as a political priority. Moreover, the declining membership (which, as shown, is also connected to these changes) put the unions in a continuously weaker bargaining position, which has made results more difficult to achieve – this making future support from the individual worker less obvious.

Concluding Remarks

The Danish flexicurity model has been an integral part of the Danish welfare regime for decades. As an institution, it has won international recognition for its ability to combine a capitalist labour market with social security. The European Union has even adopted it as a model that it encourages all member states to implement.

However, the otherwise strongly institutionalized model is on the verge of change as its security component has declined since the 1980s. The article argues that this transformation was linked to the end of the Cold War and the emergence of neoliberalism. Our arguments are rooted in a theoretical framework that explains the conditions of social groups in a society – such as the "working class" – as closely connected to external concerns of the state in question. By examining the history of "labour's" shifting importance, it has been demonstrated how the influence of "labour" has relied on deliberate political recognition and support. This support, it is argued, has been connected to the potential threat to the social order that "labour" represented.

Looking at the Danish flexicurity model in light of the above, the decline in the security dimension could be expected. The goal of unemployment benefits – namely that people can maintain relatively high living standards despite unemployment – becomes less valid discursively in a neoliberal paradigm. Looking ahead, impacts of this development are dismal. The more the protection against market fluctuations is regarded as an individual challenge (perhaps moderated by, politically sensible, active labour market policies) and political support to the collectivism that the unions represent continues to decline, the risk is not only a race to the bottom but also that the individual worker cease to regard him- or herself as a valued community member and citizen. The social dissatisfaction that follows from this will, however, not come in the form of a unified labour movement (lacking its previous support), but rather, as can be observed across Europe (Brexit being a more recent example of that), materialize as frustration, disintegration, and in support for right-wing nationalism with its supposed protection of the "little man" against globalization. The only way to prevent this development is deliberate political support for the security dimension in today's labour market.

Notes

1 Six dimensions have been assigned to the Danish model: high levels of organization with high coverage of collective agreements; nationally coordinated collective bargaining; a coordinated multi-level system; conflict and consensus; voluntarism implying autonomy with limited legal regulation; coordination between the system of negotiation and the political system (Due & Madsen 2006; Larsen & Ilsøe 2016).
2 Flexicurity as a label originated in Holland in 1995 as a political initiative to increase the flexibility of atypical types of employment and the security of the atypically employed (Andersen 2007; Crouch 2016: 192). Likewise, the Danish Model as a label first originated in the 1990s (Due, Madsen & Jensen 1993).
3 The concept of flexicurity does not have a universal definition. There is a multitude of variations of the term which are outlined in Wilthagen's so-called flexicurity-matrice (Bredgaard & Kongshøj Madsen 2015).
4 It is important to note that if the security component of the flexicurity model is removed (or drastically retrenched) it may also damage the flexibility, as increased insecurity may force the unions to demand employment protection in the form of, for instance, redundancy payments.
5 See chapter "'The making…' – af et begreb og en historie" ["'The making…' – of a concept and a history"] in Nielsen 2002: 46–49.
6 Documents from the conference are kept at the Danish labour archive (Jul Nielsen 2004). The present excerpt is translated from Danish: "at skabe den størst mulige gensidige forståelse og solidaritet mellem NATO-landenes folk… NATO (skal gøres til) et effektivt udtryk for medlemslandenes fællesskab ikke blot på det militære, men i lige så høj grad på de civile områder, der berører politiske, økonomiske og sociale problemer indenfor landene. … et militært forsvar i sig selv er ikke nok til i det lange løb at forsvare den livsform, der er det vestlige demokratis". The following excerpts – which are in US English in the original – also stem from this archive, unless otherwise stated.
7 The conclusions at the 1953 NATO conference in Copenhagen resemble the general American comprehension of the situation in the post-war years. In another context (within the "Labor Program of the Mutual Security Agency", established after the Second World War), a similar understanding is revealed, again epitomizing the attention to workers as crucial for Western survival: "We fight Russian communism on three fronts: The military, the economic, and the ideological. The working class is key to the two latter. If we lose there, we will not prevail at the military front" (Boel 1999:99; translated from Danish).
8 In Denmark during the 1990s, social democratic governments carried out most of the retrenchments of the unemployment benefits (Mailand 2010). The social democratic opposition did not manage to stop the retrenchments of the benefits in 2010 or effectively roll back the reform when elected to govern in 2011.

References

Ambjörnsson, R. 1988: *Den skötsamme arbetaren: Idéer och ideal i ett norrländskt sågverkssamhälle 1880–1930*. Stockholm: Carlsson.

Andersen, S.K. 2007: Vikarer mellem fleksibilitet og sikkerhed. *Tidsskrift for Arbejdsliv* 4:9, november 2007, 63–78.

Andersen, S.K. & J. Arnholz 2007: Hovedresultater fra projektet: Østeuropæiske arbejdere i bygge- og anlægsbranchen. *Forskningsnotat 83*. Copenhagen: Faos.

Andersen, S.K. & J. Felbo-Kolding 2013: *Danske virksomheders brug af østeuropæisk arbejdskraft*. Copenhagen: Faos.

Andersen, S.K. & B. Hansen 2007: *Mindsteløn i Europa*. Copenhagen: Faos.

Andersen, S.K. & M. Mailand 2005: *The Danish Flexicurity model: The Role of the Collective Bargaining System*. Copenhagen: Faos.

Andersen, S.K., M. Mailand & C.L. Ibsen 2012: *Den danske model i modvind*. Copenhagen: Faos.

Andersen, S.K. & K. Pedersen 2007: *Østaftalen: Individuelle østarbejdere. 1. delrapport*. Copenhagen: Faos.

Andreß, H.J. & H. Lohmann 2008: *The Working Poor in Europe: Employment, Poverty and Globalization*. Cornwall: Edward Elgar Ltd.

Baglioni, G. & C. Crouch 1990: *European Industrial relations: The Challenge of Flexibility*. London & Newbury Park: Sage Publications.

Berlanstein, L.R. 1993: *Rethinking Labor History: Essays on Discourse and Class Analysis*. Urbana: University of Illinois Press.

Boel, B. 1999: USA, EPA og vesteuropæisk fagforeningspolitik i 1950'erne. *Arbejderhistorie: Tidsskrift for historie, kultur og politik* 4, 99–111.

Boris, E. & A. Janssens 1999: *Complicating Categories Gender, Class, Race and Ethnicity*. Cambridge: Cambridge University Press.

Boserup, A. 1986: Staten, samfundet og krigen hos Clausewitz. In: N. Berg (ed.), *Carl von Clausewitz. Om Krig. Bd III: Kommentar og registre*, 911–930. Copenhagen: Rhodos.

Boserup, A. & A. Mack 1971: *Ikke-vold som nationalforsvar*. Copenhagen: Spektrum.

Boyd, K. & R. McWilliam 1995: Historical Perspectives on Class and Culture. *Social History* 20:1, 93–100.

Bræmer, M. & G. Redder 2017: Eksperter advarer: Social dumping undergraver det danske arbejdsmarked. *Ugebrevet A4,* Jan. 19, available at http://www.ugebreveta4.dk.

Bredgaard, T. & P. Kongshøj Madsen 2015: *Dansk flexicurity – fleksibilitet og sikkerhed på arbejdsmarkedet.* Copenhagen: Hans Reitzel.

Bruun, H. 1938: *Den faglige Arbejderbevægelse i Danmark indtil Aar 1900. Til ca. l880.* (Institutet Historie og Samfundsøkonomi, eds.). Copenhagen: Nordisk Forlag.

Carrier, J.G. 2015: The Concept of Class. In: J.G. Carrier, D. Kalb & A. Carbonella (eds.), *Anthropologies of Class Power, Practice and Inequality.* Cambridge: Cambridge University Press, pp. 29–40.

Carrier, J.G., D. Kalb & A. Carbonella (eds.) 2015: *Anthropologies of Class Power, Practice and Inequality.* Cambridge: Cambridge University Press.

Crouch, C. 2013: *The Strange Non-death of Neo-liberalism.* Oxford: Wiley.

Crouch, C. 2016: Flexicurity and the Crisis. In: T.P. Larsen & A. Ilsøe (eds.), *Den Danske Model set udefra: Komparative perspektiver på dansk arbejdsmarkedsregulering.* Copenhagen: Jurist- og Økonomforbundets Forlag, pp. 191–208.

Due, J. & J.S. Madsen 1993: *Labour Market Consensus: The Main Pillar of the Danish Model.* Copenhagen: Arbejdsministeriet.

Due, J. & J.S. Madsen 2006: *Fra storkonflikt til barselsfond:Den danske model under afvikling eller fornyelse.* Copenhagen: Jurist- og Økonomforbundets forlag.

Due, J., J.S. Madsen & C.S. Jensen 1993: *Den danske model: En historisk sociologisk analyse af det kollektive aftalesystem.* Copenhagen: Jurist- og Økonomforbundets forlag.

Due, J., M.D. Pihl & J.S. Madsen 2010: *Udviklingen i den faglige organisering: Årsager og konsekvenser for den danske model.* Copenhagen: Landsorganisationen i Danmark.

Eur-Lex 2007a: Access to European Labour Law, "Flexicurity – a crucial element in modernising the EU's labour market", http://eur-lex.europa.eu/legal-content/EN/ALL/?uri=URISERV:c10159. Accessed October 24, 2016.

Eur-Lex 2007b: Access to European Labour Law, "Communication from the Commission to the European Parliament, the Council, the European Economic and Social Committee and the Committee of the Regions – Towards Common Principles of Flexicurity", http://eur-lex.europa.eu/legal-content/EN/ALL/?uri=CELEX%3A52007DC0359. Accessed October 24, 2016.

European Commission & Directorate-General for Employment, I.R., and Social Affairs 2007: *Towards Common Principles of Flexicurity: More and Better Jobs through Flexibility and Security.* Luxembourg: Office for Official Publications of the European Communities.

Favell, A. 2008: The New Face of East–West Migration in Europe. *Journal of Ethnic and Migration Studies* 34:5, 701–716.

Favell, A. 2009: Immigration, Migration, and Free Movement in the Making of Europe. In: P.J. Katzenstein (ed.), *European Identity.* Cambridge: Cambridge University Press, pp. 167–189.

Friberg, J.H. 2012: The 'Guest-Worker Syndrome' Revisited? *Nordic Journal of Migration Research* 2:4, 316–324.

Hall, P.A. 1993: Policy Paradigms, Social Learning, and the State: The Case of Economic Policymaking in Britain. *Comparative Politics* 25:3, 275–296.

Hall, S. 2011: The Neo-Liberal Revolution. *Cultural Studies* 25:6, 705–728.

Hansen, R. 2003: Migration to Europe since 1945: Its history and its lessons. In: S. Spencer (ed.), *The Politics of Migration: Managing Opportunity, Conflict and Change.* Malden, Mass & Oxford, UK: Blackwell.

Harvey, D. 2005: *A Brief History of Neoliberalism.* Oxford: Oxford University Press.

Hochschild, A.R. 2016: *Strangers in Their Own Land: Anger and Mourning on the American Right.* New York: The New Press.

Højrup, T. 2003: *State, Culture, and Life-Modes: The Foundations of Life-Mode Analysis.* Aldershot, England & Burlington, VT: Ashgate.

Højrup, T., manuscript 2017: *Rethinking the Capitalist Mode of Production and Its Life-Modes.* Copenhagen.

Horgby, B. 1993: *Egensinne och skötsamhet, arbetarkulturen i Norrköping 1850–1940.* Stockholm: Carlssons.

Hyman, R. 2001: *Understanding European Trade Unionism between Market, Class and Society.* London & Thousand Oaks, Calif.: SAGE.

Ibsen, F. & H. Jørgensen 1978: *Fagbevægelse & stat.* Ålborg: Aalborg universitetsforlag.

Jensen, P.H. 2017: The Danish Flexicurity Model: Origins and Future Prospects. *Industrial Relations Journal,* forthcoming.

Jørgensen, H. 2011: *Danish "Flexicurity" in Crisis – or just Stress-Tested by the Crisis?* Berlin: Friedrich-Ebert-Stiftung, International Dialogue.

Joyce, P. 1994: *Democratic Subjects, The Self and the Social in Nineteenth-Century England.* Cambridge: Cambridge University Press.

Jul Nielsen, N. 2002: *Virksomhed og arbejderliv: Bånd, brudflader og bevidsthed på B&W 1850–1920 [Enterprise and Workers' Life: Bonds, Ruptures and Consciousness on B&W 1850–1920].* Copenhagen: Museum Tusculanum.

Jul Nielsen, N. 2004: *Mellem storpolitik og værkstedsgulv: Den danske arbejder: før, under og efter den kolde krig [Between High Politics and the Workshop Floor. The Danish Worker – Before, During and After the Cold War].* Copenhagen: Museum Tusculanum.

Jul Nielsen, N. 2013a: Arbejderen mellem praksis og ideologisering 1850–2000 [The Worker in between praxis and ideologisation 1850–2000]. *Kulturstudier* 2013:1, 58–81.

Jul Nielsen, N. 2013b: Grænseløse arbejdere – en diskussion af identitet og selvbevidsthed med udgangspunkt i polske migrantarbejdere [Borderless Workers – A discussion of identity and self-consciousness based on cases of Polish migrant workers]. *Arbejderhistorie: Tidsskrift for historie, kultur og politik*, 44–60.

Jul Nielsen, N. 2014: Ordinary Workers and Industrial Relations in a New World Order. *Sociology Study* 4:8, 728–737.

Jul Nielsen, N. 2016: Trabajadores sin fronteras: Un debate sobre identidad y autoconsciencia basado en casos de trabajadores emigrantes polacos. In: S.C. Sánchez & K. Schriewer (eds.), *Cruzando fronteras: Nuevas perspectivas sobre migración, trabajo y bienestar*. Barcelona: Edicions Bellaterra, 123–150.

Jul Nielsen, N. & M. Sandberg 2014: Between Social Dumping and Social Protection: The Challenge and Re-negotiation of Creating 'orderly working conditions' among Polish Circular Migrants in the Copenhagen Area, Denmark. *Ethnologia Europaea* 44:1, 23–37.

Kaspersen, L.B. 2012: *Denmark in the World*. Copenhagen: Gyldendal Akademisk.

Kaspersen, L.B. & N. Gabriel 2005: Survival Units as the Point of Departure for a Relational Social Theory. *Working paper*, no. 12, International Center for Business and Politics, CBS, Copenhagen.

Keune, M. & M. Jepsen 2007: *Not Balanced and Hardly New: The European Commission's Quest for Flexicurity*. Brussel: ETUI-REHS.

Kjellberg, A. & C.L. Ibsen 2016: Attacks on Union Organizing – Reversible and Irreversible Changes to the Ghent-systems in Sweden and Denmark. In: T.P. Larsen & A. Ilsøe (eds.), *Den Danske Model set udefra: Komparative perspektiver på dansk arbejdsmarkedsregulering*. Copenhagen: Jurist- og Økonomforbundets Forlag, pp. 279–302.

Kongshøj Madsen, P. 2008: Flexicurity in Danish: A Model for Labour Market Reform in Europe? *Intereconomics* 43:2, 74–78.

Kongshøj Madsen, P. 2011: Flexicurity i modvind – en analyse af den danske flexicurity-model under den økonomiske krise. *Tidsskrift for Arbejdsliv* 13:4, 8–21.

Kuhn, T.S. 1962: *The Structure of Scientific Revolutions*. Chicago: University of Chicago Press.

Larsen, T.P. & A. Ilsøe 2016: Introduktion til Den Danske Model og bogens kapitler. In: T.P. Larsen & A. Ilsøe (eds.), *Den Danske Model set udefra: Komparative perspektiver på dansk arbejdsmarkedsregulering*. Copenhagen: Jurist- og Økonomforbundets Forlag, pp. 21–51.

Levin, M.B. 1971: *Political Hysteria in America: The Democratic Capacity for Repression*. New York: Basic Books.

LiPuma, E. & B. Lee 2004: *Financial Derivatives and the Globalization of Risk*. Durham, NC: Duke University Press.

Lubanski, N. 1999: The Impact of Europeanisation on the Construction Industry – a Comparative Analysis of Developments in Germany, Sweden and Denmark. *The German Journal of Industrial Relations* 6:3, 268–291.

Lüdtke, A. 1986: Cash, Coffee-Breaks, Horseplay: Eigensinn and Politics among Factory Workers in Germany circa 1900. Hanagan, M. (ed.): *Confrontation, Class Consciousness, and the Labor Process*. New York: Greenham Press, pp. 65–95.

Mailand, M. 2010: Dagpengesystemet og flexicurity-modellen. *Faos, Forskningsnotat* 114.

Mailand, M. 2015: Dagpengereformer og flexicurity i forandring. *Faos, Forskningsnotat* 146.

Rodgers, D.T. 2011: *Age of Fracture*. Cambridge, Mass.: Belknap Press of Harvard University Press.

Schmidt, R. 2000: *Red Scare: FBI and the Origins of Anticommunism in the United States, 1919–1943*. Copenhagen: Museum Tusculanum Press.

Sennett, R. 1998: *The Corrosion of Character: The Personal Consequences of Work in the New Capitalism*. New York: Norton.

Sennett, R. 2006: *The Culture of the New Capitalism*. New Haven: Yale University Press.

Stan, S. & R. Erne 2016: Is Migration from Central and Eastern Europe an Opportunity for Trade Unions to Demand Higher Wages? Evidence from the Romanian Health Sector. *European Journal of Industrial Relations* 22:2, 167–183.

Standing, G. 2009: *Work after Globalisation: Building Occupational Citizenship*. Cheltenham: Edward Elgar.

Standing, G. 2011: *The Precariat, the New Dangerous Class*. London: Bloomsbury Academic.

Stedman Jones, G. 1983: *Languages of Class: Studies in English Working Class History, 1832–1982*. Cambridge & New York: Cambridge University Press.

Streeck, W. 2006: The Study of Organized Interests: Before "The Century" and after. In: W. Streeck & C. Crouch (eds.), *The Diversity of Democracy: Corporatism, Social Order and Political Conflict*. Cheltenham, UK & Northampton, MA: Edward Elgar, pp. 3–45.

Strøby Jensen, C. 2004: Faglig organisering under forandring: Komparative perspektiver på faglige organisationsgrader i Europa [Comparative perspectives on levels of organisation in Europe]. *Tidsskrift for arbejdsliv*, 7–25.

Wacquant, L.J.D. 2012: Three Steps to a Historical Anthropology of Actually Existing Neoliberalism. *Social Anthropology* 20:1, 66–79.

Niels Jul Nielsen, Ph.D., is an associate professor of Ethnology at the Saxo Institute, University of Copenhagen. Research themes are cultures of labour and work from the nineteenth century until today, at present with a focus on migration and the volatility of capitalism. His research is currently undertaken within the collaborative project Neoculturation of Life-Modes during the Current Transformation of State System and World Economy (lifemodes.ku.dk).
(nnielsen@hum.ku.dk)

Janus Jul Olsen has an M.A. in Public Management and Social Development from Copenhagen Business School, Denmark, and the Chinese Academy of Sciences (Sino-Danish Center). His research themes have revolved around the interlinkages between state policies, economic developments and subjectivation processes, with a comparative focus on China and Western Europe. Currently he is working as a management consultant in Denmark.
(jjol@valconconsulting.com)

WHEN THE PRESIDENT COMES
Potemkinist Order as an Alternative to Democracy in Belarus

Anastasiya Astapova, University of Tartu, Uppsala University

The Potemkin village is a metaphor for the cases of conscious, yet false construction or beautification for the sake of presenting something as better than it is, usually in front of high officials. Enumerating multiple cases and possible applications of the term (and its synonyms), I base my research on Belarus, a former Soviet and still socialist independent state governed by the same president since 1994. Going there for fieldwork at least twice a year, I noticed the extreme popularity of stories about Potemkin villages erected for the visits of the president, high officials, or foreigners. Analyzing vernacular attitudes toward Potemkinism, I argue for the multidimensional understanding of it, suggesting that in a socialist state, Potemkinist order becomes a viable alternative to democracy and a significant means for the country's self-representation.

Keywords: Belarus, Potemkin villages, post-socialism, rumor, window-dressing

The *Potemkin villages* phenomenon owes its name to what was perhaps the most famous case of building façades to hoodwink important visitors. In 1787, Catherine the Great (the Empress of Russia) departed to see her newly conquered territory of Novorossiya and Tavrida. To show this territory in the best possible way, General Grigory Potemkin ordered the construction of mock-up villages along her route. After multiple arguments, historians have agreed that this was a "myth", but this myth has not appeared out of nowhere and definitely reflects political tendencies of that time (Panchenko 1999). Much later, in the Soviet Union, *potemkinskie derevni* ("Potemkin villages") became an especially fitting idiom, a common term to refer to certain ostentatious socialist rituals concealing the real unflattering state of things. As Sheila Fitzpatrick characterized it later, "Potemkinism was a Stalinist discourse in which the defects and contradictions of the present were overlooked and the world was described not as it was but as it was becoming, as Soviet Marxists believed it necessarily *would be* [Fitzpatrick's italics] in future" (Fitzpatrick 1994: 16). Michael David-Fox also mentions Soviet *kultpokaz* ("cultural show") and *pokazuha* ("window-dressing") as a practice of showing certain ideal places – model institutions – to Western visitors: from collective farms to scientific organizations (David-Fox 2012: 98–141). Among other socialist and post-socialist countries, the Baltic states under Soviet rule (Purs 2012: 49–75) and Romania (David-Fox 2012: 100) also faced Potemkinism. Labeling contemporary Uzbekistan – another post-Soviet country – "a spectacular state", Laura Adams suggests that its government seems less concerned with Uzbek material prosperity than with its international cachet, resulting in a Potemkin-village effect for a visitor (Adams 2010: 28). These authors suggest different views on Potemkinism, while its complexity and ambiguity is, perhaps, best defined by Sheila Fitzpatrick who understands Potemkinism not just as deceitful practices for international display, but also as an envisioning of the future keeping people focused on a project.

The History and Cases of Potemkin Villages

Perhaps the most powerful Potemkinist stories circulate in the states in which socialism, as it often happens, is the foundation of the dictatorial and oppressive regime. For instance, travelers discussing North Korea often mention that the tourists are allowed to see and take pictures only of certain things there. The North Korea narrative is a good example of the very important feature of Potemkin villages: their existence is often hard to prove and stories about them remain rumors, speculations, and myths (in the same way as the narrative which initially coined window-dressing as *Potemkinism*). For example, it is often said that in order to show off their wares to the South, the North Koreans fabricated an entire village, Kijong-dong, which lies in the heavily-patrolled demilitarized zone between North and South Korea (The latest 2008). It is indeed hard to validate these rumors, which insist that the village was designed purely for show, with actors and actresses cutting the grass, turning the lights on in most buildings at the time when most people would wake up, and pretending to live happy, poverty-free lives.

Authors mention Potemkin villages with regard to various things. For instance, the journalist John Laughland criticized the trial of Slobodan Milošević, understanding it as an example of Potemkin justice and democracy, "a travesty at the heart of international justice" (Laughland 2007: 88–109). Laugland considered the trial sham, serving the aims of the major world politics actors rather than doing justice. Brian McVeigh declared window-dressing a peculiarity of Japanese higher education, with "opinions suppressed, voices lost, self-expressions discouraged, and individuality restrained" (McVeigh 2002: 3). The 2014 Sochi Olympics were often criticized for Potemkinism (Pikabu 2014). All these dimensions show how versatile the meaning of the term and its applications may be. Languages (including English) grasp this variety, producing multiple terms applicable for such cases: *window-dressing, massaging the data, building façades, beautification, mock-up, cosmetic reforms, smokescreen*, etc. Folklore, in turn, responds with humor – for instance, jokes based on the frame story "the disguised leader comes down to his people to see how they live" (Thompson 1955–1958, K1812 "King in disguise"). Below two examples from Soviet and contemporary Belarusian jokes, respectively:

Once Stalin decided to check how his people live, walked around the city, went shopping. Molotov [Bolshevik politician and diplomat] asks him, "What for? We report everything to you: people live well; they are happy... And it is not safe..." – "I will put on makeup in order to remain unrecognized." Molotov arranged goods to be brought to one of the shops and sent checklists [members of *Cheka*, the Soviet security organization] and their wives to be customers. He drove Stalin to this shop. The leader entered. He discovered that few customers bought anything. He decided to buy a hundred grams of butter, and handed in a receipt to the shop assistant. "Take more", the assistant said. "Why? I can take more tomorrow if I need." – "Fool! Tomorrow the shelves will be empty. Today this bastard is shopping, observing how his people live. That is why there are goods in the shops!" (Translated from Arkhipova & Melnichenko 2010: 278)

Lukashenko [the president of Belarus] decided to learn the truth of what his people thought about him. He disguised himself in rags and in the evening he went to the market. He went up to a butcher and asked, "How much is a kilo of meat?" – "200 roubles." – "Why is it so expensive?" – "Because our president is a jerk." The president was insulted and decided to teach this scum a lesson to scare him. Next day he came by limousine in his suit. He went to the same butcher and asked the same question. The butcher answered, "200 roubles." – "Why is it so expensive?" – "I told you yesterday, jerk!" (Male, 35, translated from the interview in Russian, recorded in 2013, Minsk)

From the point of view of classification of political jokes, suggested by Victor Raskin, such texts belong to the topic of compromising or undesirable situations coupled with the denigration of a public figure who reflects unflatteringly on the government as a whole (Raskin 1985: 235).

Maintaining faces and façades through erecting Potemkin villages is at least as old and widespread around the world as another famous piece of folklore – the fairy tale *Puss in Boots* (Uther 2004, ATU 545B). Through the course of the narrative, the cat successfully presents his master (a dowerless son of a miller) to the king. The cat hurries ahead of the king's couch and orders the country folk along the road to tell the king that the land belongs to the cat's master (saying that if they do not tell the king what he instructed them to say, he will cut them into mincemeat). As a result of these and many other manipulations, the king is impressed with the bogus son of a miller (now marquis) and his fortune, and gives him the princess in marriage. The story of window-dressing by Puss in Boots is international, as its Potemkinist elements are widespread in many cultures. Encountered everywhere, they are, however, differentially evaluated depending on the prevailing social order. Presenting and discussing this paper, I have often heard examples of Potemkinism from various countries: El Salvador, India, China, and South Africa – too many cases to retell them in this article. As Brian McVeigh argues, "all societies possess – indeed, rest upon (to some degree at least) – simulated institutions" (McVeigh 2002: 15). The difference is probably in the relevance and choice of certain institutions and objects put forward for display as they are not equally important for different branding purposes. Perhaps one of the best films to reflect on the choices of such objects is *Bienvenido, Mr. Marshall* (Spain, 1953), in which the officials try to show off Franco's Spain to U.S. emissaries in order to get financial aid from them. They consider and discuss different objects to put forward for the display, trying to demonstrate the stereotypes of Spanish culture with which the visiting American officials will be most accustomed (Noyes 2006).

The Belarusian Case: Areas of Research and Methodology

Unlike the famous Spanish movie, my study is based on reports of such performances rather than discussions of how to perform – reception rather than production. The question I focus on in this research is not about the branding process only, but about vernacular attitudes and anxieties rising around it. The focus of this article is on the attitudes toward the institutions and objects put forward for display in Belarus, a former Soviet country that elected its first president, Alexander Lukashenko, in 1994, after gaining independence in 1991. Lukashenko has ruled the country since then; for this reason, it is notorious as the last dictatorship of Europe. In addition, the country inherited a state system that was still socialist, and, unlike some other former USSR republics striving for novelties, enthusiastically preserved many of its elements in economics, politics, and everyday life. This environment appeared to be fruitful for Potemkinist practices, and, consequently, narratives, which I documented from almost every interlocutor in a series of ethnographic interviews about Belarusian political and ethnic identity as well as from constant observation and mass media research. To illustrate the Belarusian situation, I will mostly concentrate on two localities: the Vitebsk region and the so-called presidential zone – the Alexandria village and its surroundings (where Lukashenko was born and raised). The research methods used in these two localities were different. In the Vitebsk case, I held about thirty anonymous interviews. Initially, I did not aim to ask about Potemkinism, but these stories started to pop up naturally within the flow of the interview. Thus, I realized that it is an important issue in the country and I should ask and let the interlocutors talk about it as much as they find it significant.

Regarding Alexandria, the birthplace of Alexander Lukashenko, due to the special status of this presidential zone and corresponding lifestyle (perpetual Potemkinism, special attention from the ideology and security state departments, fears of those who live there), I could not reveal the true aims – researching narratives of *potemkinism* – of my visit to its citizens and record my interviews. I approached people working at various places there to have a free conversation about the places (e.g. a school), and in all our conversations, the problem of Potemkinism emerged. Being well-aware of the ethical issues of not getting consent from the interlocutors, yet, not seeing possibilities for open research, I conceal the identities of the interviewees as much as possible, to avoid harming them in any way, at the same time trying to reflect the situation without damaging its meaning.

The stories about the cases I present do not have stable emic names; most often they are referred to as *Potemkinskie derevni* and *pokazuha* (deriving from the Russian "to show"); both terms reveal pejorative connotations and were known long before Belarus became independent. Most often, the interlocutors used none of the terms though, telling no-name stories that featured the same topic of a show for the president, the bosses, or other visitors, and the first story told evoked many others. I will further refer to such cases as *Potemkin villages* (or *potemkinskie derevni*) as a vernacular term, sometimes alternating it with *Potemkinism* and *window-dressing* to avoid repetition and emphasize routinization and the omnipresence of the phenomena. Other emic keywords used in relation to these stories were *marazm* ("asininity"), characterizing the absurdness of the situation and the behavior of the higher ranks, and *neprijatnosti* ("troubles") as a threat encountered if one defies erecting the *Potemkin villages*.

It is almost impossible to say whether the stories I recorded are true or not: they remain unverified information, and the official discourse is never interested in confirming them. However, the crucial question is why and how these narrations gain meaning and enter in circulation. These rumors, of course, reflect the practice, although it is not clear how often it happens as opposed to being narrated. As Linda Dégh and Andrew Vázsonyi once suggested, "not only can facts be turned into narratives but narratives can also be turned into facts," and both types of performance become part of the oral tradition. Dégh and Vázsonyi borrow the term *ostension* from semiotics to define the cases in which the fact and the narrative get into a continuous process of retroaction, strengthening each other's viability in the paradoxical situation of coexistence (Dégh & Vázsonyi 1983: 29). The Potemkin village cases and narratives are also in an ongoing interaction, and the narratives become "maps for action", reflecting "both what has 'really' happened, but also what a person or persons can make happen" (Ellis 1989: 218). They become a form of knowledge, striving to organize a confusing world, uncovering vernacular concerns, and permitting the concealed sentiments to enter the public debate (Fine & Ellis 2010: 5, 9). After all, there is always a kernel of truth in them, although I will rather concentrate on why they become so significant that almost every interlocutor in Belarus has had his or her example for this research.

Potemkinism in Vitebsk and the Vitebsk Region

In 2010, before the presidential election, Alexander Lukashenko raised the salaries to encourage Belarusians to vote for him. For this and other economic reasons, in 2011, a serious financial crisis followed. In search of a way out, among other measures, the government tried to revive ineffective industries. As a result, in 2012, Alexander Lukashenko visited the Vitebsk woodworking enterprise, one of the financially challenged industrial units scattered around the country that became a forlorn hope during the financial crisis. Many stories accompanied and followed his visit, and, knowing some of them, I asked my interlocutors how the city had been prepared for the visit. According to the interviews, the road Lukashenko was to drive on as well as its surroundings were completely changed.

> To prepare it for Lukashenko's visit, all of the DSK [name of the district] was cleaned, moreover … they paved the road with asphalt at the very last minute, in fact, they paved the road over the snow, it was snowing for the first time… All

the workers were sent away for a day off, one line was launched, engineers and masters wearing new clothes were placed there instead of the workers, those who would not have said anything wrong. (Male, 18, recorded in Vitebsk in 2013)

And on Lukashenko's way, of course, everything was put in order. In the places where the streetlights had not worked for decades, they lit everything; they put numbers on the houses. (Female, 50, recorded in Vitebsk in 2013)

They started to pave the road with asphalt over the snow, they started to paint everything, all the roads, all the glades, even clear them of stumps; to light up the windows in every possible way; this was horrible. The head of the enterprise, which he was supposed to visit, had been fired and hired again three times. (Male, 19, recorded in Vitebsk in 2013)

The non-state, oppositionist press added to these narratives: several articles appeared claiming that during the preparations for Lukashenko's visit, trams – the main means of transportation in this district – did not work, as the road was being paved with asphalt:

Many people expressed their indignation at Vitebsk officials preparing *pokazuha* for Lukashenko. And then often added that they had not voted for him at the election; and the more things like that happened, it was more difficult to tolerate such humiliation … The façades of the houses were being painted, the trees cut, the bushes cleared, even the flowerbeds planted – no matter that it was in December. (Svaboda 2012)

Such narratives go far beyond Vitebsk. As one of the interviewees said, "Many things in our country become relevant immediately before a certain date or event." Indeed, every special event held in the country brings about new stories on the elaborate preparations for particularly important visitors. Another example comes from Polotsk, the most ancient city in the country situated in the Vitebsk region. When the city celebrated its recent anniversary and Lukashenko was supposed to come, the manhole lids were paved over with asphalt (making future access to the manholes impossible), as the workers did not have enough time to pave the road properly (as my interviewees explain). Another locally famous window-dressed building, standing on the road leading to the center of the city, is a bright pink house. As a Polotsk dweller (Male, 29) explained, the house was supposed to be demolished before the anniversary celebration, but there was not enough time for that. Since this ugly building was standing on the road Lukashenko was assumed to drive (to visit the event), it was painted pink with the sign "For sale" put on it. "Painting façades is the common practice in our country," the Polotsk interviewee concluded.

However, the façades are not painted only for the president. The former governor of Vitebsk, Alexander Kosinets (now the Head of the Presidential Administration), was infamous for multiple, often illogical changes that he launched in the city and unnecessary decorations people made in a hurry on his demands or knowing that he was coming. For instance, he forced different state institutions to adorn windows with garlands at the employees' own expense "to create a festive mood" (Female, 50, recorded in Vitebsk) before New Year:

[Did Kosinets make you decorate your building with garlands?] Yes, he issued a decree, probably unpublished, I guess on Saturday. On Sunday, people of course did not work, and did not know anything, and on their coming to work on Monday, they learned that garlands were to be there by 4 p.m., as someone would come and check that, and if the windows were not decorated, the managers would have troubles (*nepriiatnosti*). On Monday, people had to pay heaps of money for the garlands, ask their friends for them, well, as usual. (Male, 30, recorded in Minsk in 2013)

Many interviewees underlined the uselessness of such practices, which reflected the *marazm* ("asininity") of higher ranks, coming from the top and diffusing around:

They were painting the rotten old windows before the president's visit. [For *pokazuha* as well?] Of course, for *pokazuha*. I also consider that every boss has a certain *marazm* of his own level, and the higher the level is, the more *marazm* he has. (Female, 50, recorded in Vitebsk in 2013)

[Why do such cases happen?] Some idiot makes a decision, and everyone should behave the way this idiot wants. This is the style of managing coming from the very top; that is why I am not surprised at such cases flourishing at the level of the Ministry of Health or kindergartens: these are the chains of one vertical line. We just see the effect on the lower levels. (Male, 32, recorded in Minsk in 2013)

Interlocutors also notice that window-dressing is often so asinine because the qualification and profession of the officials do not correspond to the positions they occupy. One of the interviewees was retelling the story of his uncle participating in the building of an important architectural ensemble dedicated to another significant event, *Slavianski Bazaar in Vitebsk*. This music festival is held every year to promote the unity of Slavic nationalities. It always attracts many Russian visitors, including the officials of higher ranks. The city is importunately and hastily renovated every year to impress the visitors. When Alexander Kosinets visited the ensemble that was supposed to be finished before Slavianski Bazaar to amaze the guests, he was almost fully satisfied. Only one thing disturbed him, apparently: to his mind, the transformer substation supplying the ensemble with electricity was spoiling the whole composition, and he asked the employees to remove it. The employees were shocked: this caprice would cost several days of work and cause an electricity shutdown in the central district. I asked the interviewee if they objected. "Of course, not. Kosinets is a medical doctor, how will you explain it to him?" After some thinking, he added: "Well, taking into account that my uncle was demoted, maybe he objected. It may have caused *nepriiatnosti* ('troubles')" (Male, 25, recorded in Vitebsk in 2013). According to many interviews, potential troubles are the main reason of Potemkin villages being built without any objection. Thus, the craving for ideal order in Belarus often results in the contrary: fear of troubles, accusing officials of asininity, and time spent on useless decorations are hardly advantageous for actual order. Judging from the fact that the zealous advocate of decorative order, Alexander Kosinets, was promoted to the position of the Head of Presidential Administration, his politics fit the ideology of the state well.

Certain events and places in Belarus seem to have great potential for current ideology promotion and be especially apt for window-dressing. For instance, showcasing industrial enterprise becomes important during economic crisis. The anniversary celebration of the country's most ancient city, Polotsk, is significant for national identity. *Slavianski Bazaar in Vitebsk* promotes the unity of East Slavic nationalities and friendship with Russia, from which Belarus gets loans and resources. Representing the country's president – Alexander Lukashenko – in the best possible way is another important mission imposed on his birthplace.

Alexandria, the Presidential Zone

Perhaps the ultimate example of Potemkinism in Belarus is Alexandria village, the settlement where Alexander Lukashenko grew up. Extreme Potemkinism also stretches further to the so-called "presidential zone" – the surrounding villages, which Lukashenko occasionally visits (e.g. he was born in nearby Kopys' and sometimes comes to visit the hospital there). The duties of the dwellers of this cluster of villages include grooming perfect façades and undertaking elaborate preparations for each of Lukashenko's visits. Rumors about these exemplary villages and their façades circulate around the country. As one of the interlocutors joked before the trip I undertook to Alexandria and nearby villages in 2013, "even cows there do not defecate in the places not designated for defecation there" (Female, 51, recorded in Vitebsk in 2013). Moreover, alternative press keeps writing about KGB agents crowding the area and surveilling both residents and newcomers (Compromat 2006).

One of the most significant objects of the presidential zone is a museum of Lukashenko set up in the school where he studied. Calling there in advance regarding their opening hours, I learned that I would require permission to visit it. The local ideology department (a subdivision of local government subordinate to the main ideology department) grants permissions. It was possible to get permission through a phone call, but it was time consuming (the officials kept forwarding my calls and asking many questions on the aims of my visit). The museum is in fact just a room at the school, and the school's principal was the guide. The exposition is presented on four walls: the first one is dedicated to the history of the location, the one across from it is on the ethnography of the region, the third and the fourth ones, facing each other, are about Lukashenko – pictures of him and his family and some documents. Taking photos was not allowed; as the principal explained at the time, the museum was not quite ready after recent renovations, which could cause criticism and speculations in case pictures were uploaded to the Internet. Maybe the museum image was not ideal enough to become public yet. But the simplicity of the four-wall construction is already obvious. This exemplary and central touristic object-to-be must correspond to the populist appeal of Lukashenko's personal and political biography: he is from the countryside, one of the simple people (Astapova 2016). Unlike the majority of window-dressing cases described above and below, the Lukashenko museum performs humility and ordinariness. This is quite a contrast from more habitual cult of personality monuments (statues, luxurious museums, or mausoleums).

The inhabitants I met in different villages of the cluster mentioned, from the very beginning of our acquaintance, that they represent an unusual school, hospital, museum, factory or shop, as they are based in the "presidential zone". Every time Lukashenko comes to the region, they have to prepare – what if he visits them? Several people also told the same story: the principal of another school in the presidential zone was once painting its façade in a hurry and fell off the ladder breaking his leg. But, they noted, breaking the leg was for the good. Among other preparations before Lukashenko's visit (including painting the façade), the officials set up a computer class, so the principal did not suffer in vain.

However, not so many dwellers of the cluster were positive. In another institution in the presidential zone, I heard complaints that Lukashenko comes to Alexandria too often: he had been there two weeks ago and was coming again. The employees expressed their discontent: when he last came to their institution, they had to "crawl and clean everything with their bellies". On his latest arrival, they were sent to the forest, and had to stay there while he was visiting, even though it was early spring, and still frosty. A visitor from the nearby plant interjected with a comment: when Lukashenko came to his enterprise, the employees of his plant were sent to sit and wait in the warehouse in order to keep the unsightly and unreliable from the eyes of the president – to prevent a mere chance they might talk or behave inappropriately. They could say something wrong or spoil the perfect picture otherwise. Another visitor agreed: when he worked in power grids and Lukashenko was visiting a nearby factory, electricians were to stay inside the transformer substation. It happened not only because they were unsightly (as in the previous case), but to eliminate any distortion in the performance: in case the electricity was cut, they were supposed to fix it immediately. One more story he told was about the period before one of Lukashenko's re-elections when the electrician and his colleagues had received an order to hang lights in every village (and to remove them after the election). This is an example of window-dressing done by people for other people of the same social class and similar rank, ordered to make each other happier before the election, consciously and routinely completing this order.

In Alexandria and its surroundings, I never even had to ask about Potemkinism, in spite of the fears of surveillance in the presidential zone; it was the natural flow of conversation that brought the speaker to his or her complaints at the very beginning of the talk. Other visitors immediately added their examples. It was the main topic of storytelling in this locality, as all major events are dedicated to Lukashenko's arrival. The presidential zone produced a concentration of Potemkinism and a multiplicity of narratives about it.

Building a special spectacle zone around the figure of a ruler resembles a larger-scale case described by Jill Steward. The touristic image of early twentieth-century Vienna was constructed around the figure of the emperor, with the city space designed to glorify him in all possible ways. On a wider front, political events invariably reminded foreigners of the backward and troubled nature of the empire (Steward 2003: 91). Although on a smaller scale, the Alexandria village cluster, an ideal microcosm that is supposed to be the face of the country representing its president, is similarly contrasted with the narratives on how this image is really created. The ideal-to-be, artificial picture falls apart if one asks how it was painted.

Window-dressing surpasses the literal architectural enhancement and mere constructions, and is embedded into the lives of Belarusians far beyond Alexandria and Vitebsk. People even learn to benefit from it. On my recent encounter with a Belarusian scholar, telling about her doctoral dissertation on linguistics, I expressed my surprise about its easy defense: it contradicted my knowledge about the difficulties of defending a dissertation on the humanities in Belarus. "*Potemkinskie derevni*, that was what helped me," she replied. She had many English sources in her bibliography, which made her elderly professors think her dissertation was good enough. According to her, they could not read English, so they could not check these sources, but, having to maintain their academic faces, they did not confess it.

Façade performances become a priority in young families' houses. In spite of lack of money, they take bank loans for decoration and beautification of their apartments and cars; no matter that afterwards they do not have enough money for food. In a special journal issue of *Southern Folklore*, dedicated to façade performances, Dorothy Noyes suggests that in such a way "householders perform respectability through the façade, displaying both identification with and distinction within a community. The façade is a public face claimed by the family" (Noyes 1995: 91). Judging from the multiple examples, Potemkinism in Belarus becomes more than maintaining the face: it grows into the routine of everyday life.

Socialist Past and Present

A variety of reasons for Potemkinism can be found in different spheres of Belarusian life. Yet, as I will argue, the most crucial is the paternalist socialism Belarus inherited from the Soviet Union and enthusiastically promoted. The importance of the socialist past (and sometimes present) for the resurgence of Potemkinism cases and rumors is also vivid in neighboring post-Soviet countries: Russia and the Ukraine. The Belarusian narrative about paving over manholes has its variants there. Multiple pieces of news discuss paving the manholes before Vladimir Putin's arrival in Smolensk (Rosbalt 2011), Dmitry Medvedev's trip to Kirov (Lenta.ru 2009), and Victor Yanukovich's visit to Chernovtsy (TSN 2010). Looking for their origin and answering the eternal folklorist's question of whether they are the products of mono- or polygenesis fall outside of the scope of this article, but these cases seem symptomatic of the general close interrelations between socialism (or post-socialism) and Potemkinism.

In the Belarusian case, it is especially significant that being a part of the Soviet Union till 1991, the region was the window display of the Soviet system and an exemplary republic within the USSR, officially most supportive of its regime (Eke & Kuzio 2000: 537). Having gained independence, Belarus found itself at the crossroads, without clear aims, rules, or directions of development. Partially because of that, Alexander Lukashenko won the first presidential election in 1994: his appeals to the audience were similar to those made by the Soviet power and hence comprehensible. Still in need of a set of regulations, Belarusians easily adopted Lukashenko's rules of the game, including performances for the officials or foreigners. Thus, the resurgence of the rumors about Potemkin villages is not occasional. *Kultpokaz*, or *cultural show*, both for foreigners and local authorities has a revival. The foreigners are often treated in a special way also due to the long isolation of Belarusians, lasting at least since the Cold War up to now. Western travelers usually need a visa to get to Belarus (while the rest of Europe is visa-free for them); low salaries and the need to apply for visa to most countries (including the Schengen zone) do not allow Belarusians to travel and meet the foreigners outside.

One more socialist reason for Potemkinism lies in what Per Rudling calls the foundation of the modern Belarusian identity, the most influential historical event for today's Belarus – the Second World War (Rudling 2010: 9). Belarus became one of the first Soviet republics to receive the blow of the war: the country was purposefully and dramatically destroyed and almost every family lost a member. Andrej Kotljarchuk suggests that this national trauma has deeply penetrated the public discourse and self-awareness of Belarusians (Kotljarchuk 2013). Belarus was branded by ideology as a republic of partisans who fought against the Nazis, and this façade legend encouraged people to struggle during the war and enhanced the post-war development. As a country officially most supportive of the Soviet regime, after the end of the Second World War, Belarus hurriedly started to rebuild what had been destroyed. The Second World War trauma is now used to support and promote Lukashenko's ideology: current political stability is often achieved by emphasizing issues of security and giving more guarantees to the traumatized people. In the discussions of politics, many Belarusians say, "Whatever, but not a war" (*Lish by ne bylo voiny*), appealing to the national tragedy and expressing the need of certain guarantees for the sake of which they can sacrifice many other things and build Potemkin villages if necessary.

The fact that everyone participates in the creation of the façade unites people, moreover – and this is another rule of socialist politics – everyone is to some extent employed. This is an important part of the Belarusian economic system – the creation of workplaces that do not exist in the capitalist world: conductors in public transport, toilet keepers and luggage guards at the railway stations, working for low salaries. Preserving these professions performs the same function as Potemkin villages: maintaining the ideals of the socialist state and creating a feeling that every single citizen of the country has an important mission – from selling tickets in the public transport system to participating in the window-dressing process. The system becomes self-sufficient through everyone participating and being involved.

The result is what Gramsci called "excellence" – the massive production of subaltern identities of consent in highly developed hegemonies (Gramsci 1985: 61–63). Building Potemkin villages, Belarusians maintain the leader's authority and become a part – albeit subordinate – of the power bloc (Jones 2006: 58). Satisfying the hegemony's aspirations to ideal by participating in window-dressing, they achieve social guarantees – employment, free healthcare, mothers' salaries, etc. – in return. Among other consequences, Potemkinism entails the dualism of perceptions – the dichotomy of ideal and non-ideal or black and white, being very significant in the Belarusian case. It is reflected in the removal of unsightly employees and passers-by that may spoil the perfect-to-be ordered picture. Building such ideal landscapes is closely related to maintaining a standardized lifestyle, decreasing the meaning of initiative, individuality, diversity, creativity and choice – qualities that are dangerous for non-democratic societies. As a result, Potemkinism becomes a blend of both comfortable and politically correct behavior: one does not have to be creative, but just follow generally accepted scripts.

Full of contradictions, the hegemonic excellence is often subject to parody and ridicule in the narratives complaining about Potemkin villages, which are similar in their mechanisms to euphemisms, disguise, and other rituals of transcript hidden from the superior (Scott 1990). They allow a vent of emotions and prevent an open conflict. Erecting Potemkin villages and showing them off in front of the superior, one can mock the superior for believing the front afterwards. The parts in Potemkin narratives that mock the believing authorities, however, do not aim to overthrow them. As Foucault observed, power is not solely a negative restrictive force, it "also traverses and produces things. It induces pleasure, forms knowledge, produces discourse. It needs to be considered as a productive network that runs through the whole social body, much more than a negative instance whose function is repression" (Foucault 2000: 120).

The contradictions of the window-dressing can also be seen through the prism of Michael Herzfeld's notion of *cultural intimacy*:

> those aspects of cultural identity that are considered a source of external embarrassment but that nevertheless provide insiders with their assurance of common sociality, the familiarity with the bases of power that may at one moment assure the disenfranchised a degree of creative irreverence and at the next moment reinforce the effectiveness of intimidation. (Herzfeld 2005: 3)

Potemkin villages is a social practice embedded in the country's history and recognized as shameful; yet, paradoxically it gives both the feeling of commonality and the reason to disrespect the state. It results in *disemia* – the tension "between official self-presentation and what goes on in the privacy of collective introspection" (2005: 6), causing the incongruity of the façades and multiple rumors about them flooding the alternative discourse. Some tension is nevertheless worth the socialist stability provided in return.

Order of Potemkinism: Ideal Performance of the Power Falling Apart

As James Scott suggests, "the powerless are often obliged to adopt a strategic pose in the presence of the powerful and the powerful may have an interest in overdramatizing their reputation and mastery" (Scott 1990: XI), adding that "the need to deceive comes from rigor power relations" (1990: 2). In a similar vein, Dorothy Noyes claims that

> the deployment of bodies in space through the collective performance offers the occasion for the convincing realization of metaphors of order … Normative or official performances use spectacle to school us in the social order, assembling bodies to display the meaningful contrasts between them and to position them in their appropriate conceptual locations. (Noyes 1995: 98)

The Belarusian order is produced and preserved through display, reenacting rigorous power relations in "the last dictatorship of Europe". The state and its representatives occupy all spheres of life, with the ideology and politics penetrating culture and economics. The functions of these spheres are distorted, and they start to play the ideological role not characteristic of them. One of the many results, described by Alexander Sarna, is turning certain architectural objects into shock works (*udarnye stroiki*), attaching their completion to the certain dates (Sarna 2008: 246), which, in turn, harms the quality of the buildings as well as their reputation. They are immediately surrounded by rumors and doubts, which are hardly positive for the regime that initially used this way of erecting buildings as propaganda (2008: 247). Another example of ideology penetrating various landscapes is the Alexandrian case. The perfection of the otherwise ordinary Belarusian village aims to metonymically transfer the ideal qualities of this subject territory to their leader by proxy. Reinforcing his power through Potemkinism, Lukashenko performs what Jean Baudrillard calls "seduction" – the willful neglect of truth in favor of the play of power and creation (Baudrillard 1991).

Another idea of Baudrillard – that of *simulacrum* masking, perverting, or even replacing the profound reality – also seems suitable in the Belarusian case. Particular for postmodernity, simulacrum precedes the original, with the distinction between reality and representation erased as a result (Baudrillard 1994: 6, 16–17). Baudrillard refers to the words credited to Ecclesiastes: "The simulacrum is never that which conceals the truth – it is the truth which conceals that there is none. The simulacrum is true" (1994: 1). In Belarus, the simulacrum of order becomes a viable political model, arousing as many contradictions in the vernacular attitudes as any other – democratic or dictatorial regime.

Potemkin Villages and Narratives about them: Conformism or Passive Resistance?

One of the major questions regarding the study of socialism and Soviet countries in particular, emerging in almost every scholarly piece of writing on the subject, is whether people resist or enjoy the practices documented. It is not only the socialist cases that demand the answer though. For instance, in his book *Exit, Voice and Loyalty: Responses to Decline in Firms, Organizations, and State*, Albert Hirschman suggests that in case customers of economic enterprises or citizens of political systems are dissatisfied with these enterprises or systems, they act in three possible ways. They exit (or immigrate), voice their dissatisfaction, or remain loyal to what they do not like due to different reasons (Hirschman 1970). The latter idea is, perhaps, the most well-developed in socialist studies, and the notion of *Ketman*, formulated by a Polish poet of Lithuanian origin, Czesław Miłosz, is one of the most characteristic for this approach. Miłosz offers the term *Ketman* for the acts of paying lip service to authority and sacrificing the possibility of objecting and protesting for the sake of professional development or personal survival (Miłosz 1953: 54–81). Developing this idea later, Erving Goffman adds that "the cynic, with all his performance disinvolvement, may obtain unprofessional pleasures from his masquerade, experiencing a kind of gleeful spiritual aggression from the fact that he can toy at will with something his audience must take seriously" (Goffman 1956: 10). To give an example similar to *Ketman* and advantages the inferiors may achieve from *Ketman*, James Scott mentions Laotians, who responded to the requirement made by French officials to have a village headman by creating a set of bogus notables who had no local influence and who were presented to colonial functionaries as the local officials. Scott calls such cases *ersatz façades,* erected in order to shield another reality from detection (Scott 1990: 132). Such performances in the front give licenses in the back; meanwhile fooling the superior is an incomparable pleasure. This empirical example shows how much more multidimensional the cases of Potemkin villages are than their potential theoretical descriptions based on the monosemantic approaches.

Another example comes from the formerly socialist Albanian capital Tirana. When it got a new mayor, Edi Rama, in 2000, he initiated steady changes in the capital, seeking to transform its face of "an orderly but dull capital city" (Makgetla 2010: 3) by, first of all, painting grey Soviet-style apartments and government buildings in bright colors and artistic designs. This is the way he chose to deal with the legacy of the Marxist-Leninist dictatorship and the further transitional period of Albania: hundreds of illegally constructed buildings, shady neighborhoods, and generally poor infrastructure. Not everyone agreed with Rama's strategies (some accused him of cosmetic reforms), but the public debate about it signaled a growing civic involvement, a critical shift in citizens' perceptions of government and their role in it (Makgetla 2010).

Negative views, of course, form a large part in window-dressing discourse, and the oppositional press often employ them to launch its critique of the government. For example, according to one of the Belarusian articles by the non-governmental press, a road hurriedly paved with asphalt before the harvesting celebration, in Gorki, Mogilev region (again, Lukashenko was supposed to come there), collapsed, and a family of three fell through the ground and were injured (Novoteka 2013). However, usually the cases of window-dressing have more than one dimension, even in the perception of one person.

For instance, when it comes to Kosinets' aforementioned changes in Vitebsk, attitudes toward them are ambiguous. While his order to stub the trees that veterans planted on the Victory Square long ago is often criticized, on the other hand, it is appreciated that the Square nowadays has facilities for entertaining children. This view is visible in the following excerpt of one interview:

> About the changes in the city, my attitude is ambivalent: on the one hand, the city became attractive, places for rest appeared, on the other hand, spaces that were too important, like the Victory square, were rebuilt. But the young people are

happy, children are happy… Also, just before Lukashenko's visit, the car hit the fence [the fence became unsightly for Lukashenko coming by], so the fence was expanded, and it was positive. (Male, 42, recorded in Vitebsk in 2013)

And this is the conclusion about Potemkinism from another interviewee:

[Are there many cases of *pokazuha*?] Of course, there is a lot of *marazm*. But I think it happens not only in Belarus, in all the countries, it was and will be like that. (Male, 20, recorded in Minsk in 2013)

Similarly, the aforementioned Alexandrian case with the principal who was painting the school in a hurry and broke his leg is symptomatic: many concluded that the leg of the school principal was broken not in vain, since the school got computers. Moreover, people learn not only to survive, but to benefit from such a system, as was shown in the case of the dissertation easily defended because professors did not know English, but could not confess it, having to maintain their academic faces.

These and other cases I encountered during my fieldwork confirm the necessity of viewing socialist realities more broadly than in terms of dichotomies. Statistical research, with its answer options of "I support the Potemkinism" and "I reject it", is hardly applicable here. It is the folkloristic methods of open interview and analysis that show how polyvocal the whole picture is, how many pros and cons coexist in the view of one person. It resembles the idea of vernacular religion proposed by Leonard Primiano to put an end to the two-tiered understanding of religion (Primiano 1995). To paraphrase it, vernacular attitudes toward the political are more than mere conformism or resistance. In the same way as the worldview of one person may accommodate beliefs institutionalized as pagan and Orthodox, political acceptance and resistance may peacefully coexist mixed together due to different reasons – security, benefits, approval, etc. Conformism and resistance paradoxically coexist in building Potemkin villages and stories about them.

In his argument against dichotomies in socialist studies, Alexei Yurchak touches upon a similar paradox. Writing about the late Soviet Union, he notices that "reproducing the system and participating in its continuous internal displacement were mutually constitutive processes" (2006: 283). Similarly, in Belarus, the constant reproduction of the performance of window-dressing finds its displacement in rumors and dissatisfaction with the system being reproduced. The more ordered the life is by the state, the more it decays, cracks and mismatches. In its turn, the outlet of negative emotions and dissatisfaction allows reproduction of window-dressing.

Potemkinism has many dimensions: positive evaluations of window-dressing peacefully coexist with the negative ones even in the same interview. As Erving Goffman suggests, "an individual may be taken in by his own act or be cynical about it. These extremes are something a little more than just the ends of the continuum. Each provides the individual with a position which has its own particular securities and defenses" (Goffman 1956: 11). Placing oneself in a particular position on the continuum, one takes multiple criteria into account: safety, comfort, professional development and political views. It is important to keep in mind that Potemkin villages do not always have a pejorative connotation: they are controversial.

Potemkin Villages and the Problem of (Mis-)Representation

The ideal Potemkinist order does not hold the same kind of value for the insiders and the others: a more abstract form of social guarantees for the former, it is more of a visual display for the latter. Potemkinism is a good tool for foreign propaganda, targeting mainly the values of a nostalgic post-Soviet audience. The self-representation in front of most post-Soviet countries becomes extremely important since these are also the main partners in economic and political cooperation. Most of the Belarusian trade or military unions, agreements on cooperation in education, healthcare, law and other spheres of life were signed with them. And Belarus seems to succeed in its play in front of its target audience. During my trips around former Soviet countries (e.g. in the Caucasus, Central Asia, Russia), people always address me to express their positive attitude toward Lukashenko's politics, and especially the order he established. But the main spectator is certainly Russia – the neighbor, political and economic partner, resource-supplier, and investor of Belarus. In 2007–2010, when I lived in St. Petersburg, almost everyone asked me why I was not living in Belarus, the country of my citizenship. Their surprise was based on their own visits to Belarus and seeing clean broad streets, green parks and "order" all around. This order conflicted with chaotic St. Petersburg or other Russian cities, and caused the general opinion on Belarus as a well-regulated country among Russians who were nostalgic about visual stability and the Soviet Union. As a result, both in Russia and some other post-Soviet countries, phrases like "*Bat'ka* [father] keeps the country in order" or "We need *Bat'ka* [father] to establish order [*navesti poriadok*] in Russia" became almost idioms. Lukashenko's nickname *Bat'ka* and his *poriadok* are now the keywords to define Belarus. The sterile green streets taken at face value have become synonymous with order.

Belarus is successful at building façades for the particular audience most important for Belarusian well-being: plenty of Russians come to the well-ordered Belarus for tourism and shopping. The general friendship of Russia with Belarus as a "stable country" is beneficial for the latter, as Potemkin order brings Russian visitors, investments, and gas. Belarusian solid façades are especially highly appreciated in contrast with the current Ukrainian situation: unlike the Ukraine (another country regarded as East Slavic), Belarus is sturdy not only in its order, but also in its friendlier position toward Russia. The performance hits the audience relevant for the current political regime and economic situation. Moreover, it maintains the image of Lukashenko as a serious and consistent president.

Conclusion

Among other definitions of 'order', the Merriam-Webster dictionary suggests two contradicting ones: order is "the state of peace, freedom from confused or unruly behavior, and respect for law or proper authority" and "a specific rule, regulation, or authoritative direction" (Merriam-Webster). The second, rather Potemkinist understanding of order is antonymous to the first, rather Western definition. Order as a command in Belarus becomes an alternative to the order as peace. This state of things seems to constitute a viable social model in Belarus, contrasting Western-style democracies often imposed as a norm. It is not freedom or democracy that counts in the Belarusian case, but power: the ability of the leader to provide peace, prosperity, and stability. From the country's early history, Potemkinist order in Belarus was planted into the fertile ground of contemporary socialism, supported by Soviet templates, national trauma, and the paternalist state with its set of reliable rules.

It is not surprising that the ideal artificial order sometimes cracks: people tell cheerful jokes about Lukashenko's visits, the humorous rumors about presidential visits circulate all over the country, etc. At the same time people learn to adapt and benefit from the situation they find themselves in, to compromise for the sake of socialist advantages they are given and familiar with. Building Potemkin villages is an insignificant sacrifice if one receives free medical aid, education, and other benefits of the socialist state in return, especially for a person who is used to it and has never lived in another political system. Erecting the Potemkin villages becomes everyday life and regular routine, going far beyond the architectural enhancements for the state.

What is more, Potemkin order easily finds its thankful target audience, that is, former Soviet states, which on their tough post-socialist way to democracy are often nostalgic of past visual stability of the Soviet Union. The visually ordered country is pleasant to deal with when it comes to investments or other deals. Both people and the state learned Potemkin pragmatics and the ways to benefit from it. No wonder that appearance of peace and stability become more important than actual peace and stability in this part of the world: the Belarusian brand of an ordered and reliable country works when it is promoted to both domestic and foreign spectators.

References

Adams, Laura L. 2010: *The Spectacular State: Culture and National Identity in Uzbekistan.* Durham: Duke University Press.

Arkhipova, Alexandra & Mikhail Melnichenko 2010: *Jokes about Stalin: Texts, Comments, Research* (published in Russian). Moscow: OGI.

Astapova, Anastasiya 2016: Political Biography: Incoherence, Contestation, and the Hero Pattern Elements in the Belarusian Case. *Journal of Folklore Research* 53:2, 31–62.

Baudrillard, Jean 1991: *Seduction.* New York: Palgrave Macmillan.

Baudrillard, Jean 1994: *Simulacra and Simulations.* Michigan: University of Michigan Press.

Compromat 2006: *In Alexandria, Lukashenko's Relatives Ruin Themselves with Drinking* (published in Russian), http://www.compromat.ru/page_19633.htm. Accessed August 15, 2014.

David-Fox, Michael 2012: *Showcasing the Great Experiment: Cultural Diplomacy and Western Visitors to the Soviet Union, 1921–1941.* Oxford & New York: Oxford University Press.

Dégh, Linda & Andrew Vázsonyi 1983: Does the Word 'Dog' Bite? Ostensive Action as Means of Legend Telling. *Journal of Folklore Research* 20:1, 5–34.

Eke, Steven M. & Taras Kuzio 2000: Sultanism in Eastern Europe: The Socio-Political Roots of Authoritarian Populism in Belarus. *Europe-Asian Studies* 52:3, 523–547.

Ellis, Bill 1989: Death by Folklore: Ostension, Contemporary Legend, and Murder. *Western Folklore* 48:3, 201–220.

Fine, Gary Alan & Bill Ellis 2010: *The Global Grapevine: Why Rumors of Terrorism, Immigration, and Trade Matter.* Oxford: Oxford University Press.

Fitzpatrick, Sheila 1994: *Stalin's Peasants: Resistance and Survival in the Russian Village after Collectivization.* New York: Oxford University Press.

Foucault, Michael 2000: *Essential Works of Foucault 1954–1984. Vol. 3. Power.* New York: New Press.

Goffman, Erving 1956: *The Presentation of Self in Everyday Life.* Edinburgh: University of Edinburgh.

Gramsci, Antonio 1985: *Selections from the Cultural Writings.* London: Lawrence & Wishart.

Herzfeld, Michael 2005: *Cultural Intimacy: Social Poetics in the Nation-State.* New York & London: Routledge.

Hirschman, Albert O. 1970: *Exit, Voice, and Loyalty: Responses to Decline in Firms, Organizations, and States.* Cambridge, MA: Harvard University Press.

Jones, Steve 2006: *Antonio Gramsci.* London & New York: Routledge.

Kotljarchuk, Andrej 2013: World War II Memory Politics: Jewish, Polish and Roma Minorities of Belarus. *The Journal of Belarusian Studies* 7:1, 7–37.

Laughland, John 2007: *Travesty: The Trial of Slobodan Milosevic and the Corruption of International Justice.* London: Pluto Press.

Lenta.ru 2009: *For Medvedev's Arrival in Kirov the Railway Road was Paved* (published in Russian), May 15, http://lenta.ru/news/2009/05/15/meet/. Accessed August 15, 2014.

Makgetla, Tumi 2010: A New Face for a Tired City: Edi Rama and Tirana, Albania, 2000–2010. *Innovations for Successful Societies,* http://www.princeton.edu/successfulsocieties/content/data/policy_note/PN_id135/Policy_Note_ID135.pdf. Accessed August 15, 2014.

McVeigh, Brian J. 2002: *Japanese Higher Education as Myth.* Armink, New York: M.E. Sharpe.

Merriam-Webster: *Order,* http://www.merriam-webster.com/dictionary/order. Accessed August 15, 2014.

Miłosz, Czesław 1953: *The Captive Mind.* New York: Knopf.

Novoteka 2013: *In Gorki a Married Couple Fell through the Paving* (originally published in Russian), http://www.novoteka.ru/seventexp/5897836, January 7. Accessed August 15, 2014.

Noyes, Dorothy 1995: Façade Performances in Catalonia: Display, Respect, Reclamation, Refusal. *Southern Folklore* 52, 97–120.

Noyes, Dorothy 2006: Waiting for Mr. Marshall: Spanish American Dream. In: Alexander Stephan (ed.), *The Americanization of Europe: Culture, Diplomacy, and Anti-Americanism after 1945.* New York & Oxford: Berghahn Books, pp. 307–336.

Panchenko, Alexander 1999: Potemkin Villages as a Cultural Myth. In: Alexander Panchenko, *Russian History and Culture: The Works of Different Years* (published in Russian). Saint-Petersburg: Una, pp. 462–475.

Pikabu 2014: *Potemkin Villages in Sochi* (published in Russian), http://pikabu.ru/story/potemkinskie_derevni_v_sochi_ili_olimpiyskaya_butaforiya_dlinnopost_1901220. Accessed August 15, 2014.

Primiano, Leonard Norman 1995: Vernacular Religion and the Search for Method in Religious Folklife. *Western Folklore* 54:1, 37–56.

Purs, Aldis 2012: *Baltic Façades: Estonia, Latvia and Lithuania since 1945.* London: Reaktion books.

Raskin, Victor 1985: *Semantic Mechanisms of Humor.* Dordrecht, Boston & Lancaster: D. Reidel.

Rosbalt 2011: *The Manholes Were Paved for Putin's Arrival* (published in Russian), http://smolenskobl.ru/news/news216043.php. Accessed August 15, 2014.

Rudling, Anders Per 2010: Lukashenko and Red-Browns: State Ideology, Respect to the Past, and Political Belonging (published in Belarusian). *Palityčnaja Sfiera* 14, 90–113.

Sarna, Alexandr 2008: Politics and Symbol: Strategies of Political Marketing in Belarus 2004–2006. In: Almira Usmanova (ed.), *Belarusian Format: Invisible Reality* (published in Russian). Vilnius: EHU, pp. 232–264.

Scott, James C. 1990: *Domination and the Arts of Resistance: Hidden Transcripts.* New Haven & London: Yale University Press.

Steward 2003: The Potemkin City: Tourist Images of Late

Imperial Vienna. In: Felix Driver & David Gilbert (eds.), *Imperial Cities: Landscape, Display, and Identity*. New York & Manchester: Manchester University Press, pp. 78–95.

Svaboda 2012: *The Trams were Stopped in Vitebsk: The Asphalt is Paved for Lukashenko* (published in Belarusian), December 4, http://www.svaboda.org/content/article/24788628.html. Accessed August 15, 2014.

The latest 2008: *A Dictatorship's Delights,* June 20, http://www.the-latest.com/a-dictatorships-delights. Accessed August 15, 2014.

Thompson, Stith 1955–1958: *Motif-index of Folk-Literature: A Classification of Narrative Elements in Folktales, Ballads, Myths, Fables, Mediaeval Romances, Exempla, Fabliaux, Jest-Books, and Local Legends.* Revised and enlarged edition. Bloomington: Indiana University Press.

TSN 2010: *Manholes were Paved before Yanukovich's Arrival in Chervovtsy*, August 9, http://ru.tsn.ua/ukrayina/v-chernovcah-k-priezdu-yanukovicha-zaasfaltirovali-kanalizacionnye-lyuki.html. Accessed August 15, 2014.

Uther, Hans-Jörg 2004: *The Types of International Folktales: A Classification and Bibliography. Based on the system of Antti Aarne and Stith Thompson*. FF Communications no. 284–286. Helsinki: Suomalainen Tiedeakatemia.

Yurchak, Alexei 2006: *Everything was forever, until it was No More: The Last Soviet Generation*. Princeton: Princeton University Press.

Anastasiya Astapova is a research fellow at the Department of Estonian and Comparative Folklore, University of Tartu (Estonia), and a Swedish Institute visiting fellow at the Institute of Russian and Eurasian Studies, Uppsala University (Sweden). She has done fieldwork and published extensively on humor, rumor, and nationalism. Her recent activities include fieldwork among refugees and asylum-seekers in Estonia, and participation in the COST Action project "Comparative Analysis of Conspiracy Theories".
(anastasiya.ast@gmail.com)

"WE ASKED FOR WORKERS. WE GOT BUREKS INSTEAD"
Meanings and Material Significance of the Burek in Slovenia

Jernej Mlekuž, Research Centre of the Slovenian Academy of Sciences and Arts

The dish *burek* was brought to Slovenia by people from the other republics of the Socialist Federal Republic of Yugoslavia (SFRY) in the 1960s. It is now the handiest and most frequently used signifier in Slovenian popular culture, media, vernacular language etc. for immigrants from the former republics of the SFRY, the Balkans, the SFRY itself and the phenomena associated with it. This paper addresses why and how this semantic hyperinflation occurred to precisely this fast food. The burek is a product of Slovenian nationalism *par excellence* and cannot be understood without taking into consideration the material conditions of the object. The paper shows that the burek plays a significant role in the formation and reproduction of identities.

Keywords: material culture, meanings, nationalism, burek, Slovenia

The Unleashed Burek

In the first open-source online dictionary of spoken Slovene, *Razvezani jezik* (The Unleashed Tongue), the *burek* – an important, frequently prepared and eaten dish among many immigrants and their descendants in Slovenia and also Slovenia's popular fast food – is described as follows:

> In the vernacular a burek also means an idiot or an incompetent [person]. Example: "*You're a bunch of complete bureks!*" Of course this pejorative use contains slightly veiled chauvinism or racism; a burek in this sense implies a stupid and incompetent southerner, a person from the Balkans or the Orient. (Razvezani jezik 2012)

The large majority of users of this phraseme are probably not aware of this "slightly veiled chauvinism or racism". In some cases, for instance among certain (secondary-school) peer groups, it can even be a term of endearment. However, it is clearly not a term of endearment in the song "Ti si burek" ("You're a Burek") by the national folk-music group Trio Genialci. In the popular video (at least judging by YouTube views),[1] a well-heeled Slovenian businesswoman comes home to find her immigrant husband (ostensibly a Bosnian) on the couch wearing a singlet and track suitbottoms, with a beer and a remote in his hands, his feet on the table, football on the telly, a baby in the corner needing its diaper changed and her husband's brother also on the couch, also with a beer in his hand. As she throws him out of the house, she sings the following refrain:

> You're a burek, a burek squared
> And instead of me, put a rope around your neck
> You're a burek, a burek squared
> But why was it me you fooled that time
> Get your stuff and get out of here.
> (Trio Genialci 2008)

The burek has therefore made its way into not just Slovenian hands, mouths and streets, but the Slovene language as well. And in no small measure: "Burek? Nein, danke" – probably Slovenia's most well-known and frequently reproduced graffito (in this and the following statements the burek again signifies, connotes, stands for immigrants, the Balkans etc.); "Burek? Ja, bitte" – the title of at least two articles in prominent Slovenian newspapers; "Anti Burek Sistem" (or A.B.S.) – the name of a project by the skinhead group SLOI; "I'll have a burek, but not a mosque" – another popular Slovenian graffito; "you don't have enough for a burek" – a very frequently used slang expression meaning "you have no idea" or "you're clueless", similar to "you're a burek" or "you're a burek squared"; my own book *Burek.si!?* (Mlekuž 2008a) an academic work which owing to the "triviality" and probably also the "significance" of the object of study triggered numerous discussions and vehement responses among the general public. These examples are only a few of the more noticeable media and pop-culture roles played by the rolled or folded dish, filled with all sorts of fillings, and having the status of an increasingly naturalized "immigrant" from the Balkans. And it is precisely its immigrant status which has to the greatest extent formed its current meaning in Slovenia. Slovenia was the most industrially developed republic of the former Socialist Federal Republic of Yugoslavia (SFRY), and therefore attracted the highest proportion of immigrants from the other Yugoslav republics (see Josipovič 2006, 2012). This led to heated nationalism in the decade before and after Slovenia gained its independence (1991), which was in great measure focused on immigrants from the SFRY, who had formerly been fellow countrymen but were now "foreigners" (see Pajnik 2002). But why and how did the burek inspire so much semantic richness, so many different meanings – however predominantly attached to nationalism and its need for a culinary Other?

In seeking an answer to this question, this article starts with the fundamental idea of modern studies of material culture: that materiality is an integral part of culture and society, and that culture and society cannot be understood outside of materiality. To focus more closely: the meanings of objects cannot be understood (solely) as a product of discourses and signifying practices, but must be looked at (also) as embedded in the objective, material domain, in numerous complex ways. The investigation of meanings does not entail the negation or elimination of materiality.

Thus, the article does not deal with the meaning of things in general, but specifically with the meanings of material culture, of objects. As Daniel Miller (1994: 397) says: "the phrase the 'meaning of things' (…) tends to implicate something beyond the narrow question of semanticity by which artefacts, like words, might have sense and reference. Rather, the notion of meaning tends to incorporate a sense of 'meaningful' closer to the term 'significance'." When we speak of the meaning of objects, continues Miller (1994: 397), the main emphasis is more connected "with questions of 'being' rather than questions of 'reference'." This article explores how the meanings of the burek, the question of its semanticity, is connected or intertwined with the question of its significance. It argues that when investigating the meaning of the burek, questions of "reference" should be dialectically confronted with questions of "being". Thus, the sense and reference of the burek will be observed through the optics of its significance.

The question of the "being" or significance of objects leads to the central idea of a "material turn". According to the key theorists, objects are significant in relation not so much to what they *mean* (the semiotic) as to what they *do* (cf. Gell 1998; Miller 1987, 1998, 2010). Such an approach, following Alfred Gell (1998: 6) could also be called an "'action'-

centred approach", that is "preoccupied with the practical mediatory role of (…) objects in the social process, rather than with interpretation of objects 'as if' they were text." Thus the article also argues that the burek not only represents or reflects meaning, but also intervenes, makes a difference, and alters people's minds.

The article is based on a very wide range of materials (50 conversations with burek consumers and other people associated with bureks, such as burek stand owners and specific burek consumers, mostly youth groups in the past and present), periodicals and websites, (pop-)cultural and other products, participant observation with some selected groups (e.g. secondary-school peer groups consuming "ultragreasy bureks" (see Mlekuž 2017), collected primarily in the years 2005–2007 for a Ph.D. thesis, as well as less intensively collected newer materials (mostly periodicals and websites), that have not been part of any specific research project.

On the Dining Table and on the Street

The burek – a pastry made of phyllo dough with various fillings, well-known in the Balkans, in Turkey[2] (*bürek*) and under other names in the Near East, came to Slovenia with immigrants from the republics of the SFRY in the 1960s (which according to the 1981 census made up 5.4%, and according to the 1991 census 7.6% of the population of Slovenia, and the large majority of whom came to Slovenia as migrant labourers [Josipovič 2006]). Slovenia, the most industrially ambitious republic in the SFRY, needed a workforce. And with that workforce – with immigrants from the former republics of the SFRY – came the burek. To paraphrase Max Frisch's well-known epigram: We asked for workers. We got bureks instead.[3]

The burek was and still is frequently prepared and eaten by immigrants from the former republics of the SFRY and their descendants in Slovenia. But what stands out is its vital role in the manifestation and constitution of the society and culture of Muslim immigrants from Bosnia and Herzegovina, and to a somewhat lesser extent among other immigrants of the Muslim faith, in Slovenia. The differences appear first of all in appellation. While the great majority of ethnic and other communities from the former SFRY use the word burek to signify a dish made of phyllo dough filled with various meat, cheese, vegetable and fruit fillings, the inhabitants of Bosnia and Herzegovina are not inclined to use the word burek so broadly. They use the word burek to signify a dish made of phyllo dough filled (only) with meat. And this dish is a part of a group of pies which also includes the *sirnica* (cheese filling), *krumpiruša* (potatoes), *zeljanica* (spinach), *kupuspita* (cabbage), *pita sa tikvom* or *tikvenuša/masirača* (squash), etc. Furthermore, the burek and the other pies are irreplaceable elements of various religious, life- and other events, such as *iftar*, "an evening meal during the fasting month of Ramadan", Bosnian Muslim holidays, weddings, etc. The burek is therefore an important companion to rites of passage. And here it should be mentioned that the majority of the negative connotations that the burek has in the stylistic figures of the Slovene language, and with which I introduced this text, are in direct contrast to the meanings the burek has in Bosnia and Herzegovina – the land of the burek "numero uno" – where it is associated with homeliness, warmth, safety and sociability. The place of the burek in Bosnia and Herzegovina was explained quite nicely by Bosnian pop star Dino Merlin when asked why he had called his album *Burek*:

> I wanted to show the burek on the symbolic level as one of our culturally valued objects, but similar to a man who walks past his wife every day without seeing her beauty, we are not aware of its value. So we have all of this, but we don't know it. Something that has been verified as good for centuries is defined as high-quality, classic and art. That is, only those things that survive for centuries are worthy of appreciation and epithets such as "classic" and "art". The burek is both an authentically Bosnian and an anti-globalist phenomenon. (Cited in Bikić 2004: 10)

Immigrant families in Slovenia treat the burek not as a mere commodity; it is eaten by people who make it themselves and serve it to family and friends. The participants in the exchange of a homemade burek see it as a gift or an expression of hospitality. The circulation of homemade bureks and on the other hand the production and consumption of industrial, bakery-made and street bureks demonstrates the difference between a gift economy and a market economy (see Gregory 1982; Mauss 1954) or, to use Appadurai's (1986) definition, "regimes of value", between which there is very little common dialogue.

Also more than obvious is the conceptual and contextual difference between making and eating bureks and other pies within immigrant families, that is bureks which elude the market, and bureks which were given life by the market economy. In the majority of immigrant families, bureks are prepared and eaten as the main daily meal, either lunch or dinner, and thus support the traditional and most likely also still the dominant family meal structure. Commodity bureks – at least street bureks, that is *fast food* bureks – in the majority of cases resist this traditional dominant meal structure. They are usually eaten "on the run" – more subordinate to hunger than to a seated meal – and unlike in immigrant families, where bureks or pies are served on a plate and eaten with utensils, always wrapped in paper and eaten with one's hands. In immigrant families bureks are a relatively traditional dietary element, closely connected with the cultural tradition, while commodity bureks, at least on urban streets, in Slovenian bakeries and shops, are something of a novelty, which the majority of ethnic Slovenes have known for no more than three or four decades. The space, distance, and limited communication between these two economic spheres or contexts are also borne witness to by the fact that the great majority of immigrants, primarily of the Muslim faith, from the former SFRY with whom I had conversations and who make bureks and other pies several times a week, had never in their entire lives in Slovenia tried a bakery-made, industrial or street burek. And most probably, if burek stands run by Albanians from Macedonia had not appeared in Slovenia in the 1960s and if bureks had not been introduced by local bakeries and industrial food producers in the 1990s (nowadays the majority of bureks produced in Slovenia are made in "Slovenian" bakeries and industrial food plants), the majority of less adventuresome Slovenes would never have heard of the burek. At least not in Slovenia.

Following Raymond Williams (2005: 40–41), I could say that among immigrant families, the burek is a part of a residual culture which is significantly removed from the dominant culture. By "residual", Williams (2005: 40) means that "some experiences, meanings and values, which cannot be verified or cannot be expressed in terms of the dominant culture, are nevertheless lived and practiced on the basis of the residue – cultural as well as social – of some previous social formation." The emergent meanings of the burek, however, stand to a large degree in opposition to these residual meanings, particularly those that are employed in the dominant culture. On the level of meanings there are two more or less op-

Ill. 1: Fast food burek. Photo by the author, Ljubljana 2015.

posite positions with respect to the burek, with very little common dialogue: the unincorporated residual culture (the burek among immigrants) and the incorporated emergent culture (the burek among non-immigrants, subject to various discourses, primarily nationalistic, about which more will be said below, and healthy-lifestyle discourses, about which more has been said elsewhere [Mlekuž 2008a, 2017]).[4]

Today, the burek has worked its way deep into the Slovenian dietary mainstream. According to a newspaper survey from 2005, it ranks among the most popular fast foods or street foods in Slovenia, and in urban areas it is even the most popular fast food.[5] It is also probably the champion, at least among fast foods or street food, with respect to quantitative growth in production and consumption, and in the category of expansion into numerous new areas and institutions. Nowadays the burek can be found not just on the streets of Slovenia's towns or hiding in immigrant (and increasingly non-immigrant) kitchens. In fact, it is stealing shelf space from other deep-frozen items in the freezers of Slovenian (super)markets (it is produced in both frozen and non-frozen form by Slovenia's two largest industrial bakeries), eaten by the Slovenian Army, enjoyed as a snack in Slovenian schools (but no more than once a month), appears at numerous formal and informal parties and events, is served on certain flights of the Slovenian national airline, is delivered in trucks carrying Slovenian-made goods to foreign markets etc. Which again does not mean that doors everywhere are open to bureks, much less wide open. For instance, they are almost completely ignored by general, broad-format "Slovenian" cookbooks written for or adapted to Slovenian cooks. In a survey of thirty cookbooks, only one of them contained a recipe for burek. This disavowal of burek-recipes in the "sacred", highly selective and controlled world of books is all the more striking in contrast to the plethora of recipes found in the "profane" periodical press and above all on websites. On Slovenia's most popular culinary website Kulinarika.net can thus be found a full 44 recipes for burek, which places it among the most popular dishes in Slovenia (of course it is very difficult to compare the relative popularity of different dishes, but if we compare it just with its fast-food rival the hamburger, the latter falls far behind with just 9 recipes).[6] This will also be touched on below. But first it is worth discussing how the burek became a part of this, what Williams calls incorporated emergent culture and what its place is within that culture.

Calories and Symbols

According to interviews with burek producers and consumers, and newspaper articles, street bureks were eaten primarily by immigrants all the way up to the 1980s. At that time, the burek started being eaten by non-immigrants, usually those who, according to Peter Stanković (2005: 36), were not drawn to nationalist "euphoria" and the "Yugophobia" associated with it.[7] In the 1980s, after the death of Tito (1980), Yugoslavia found itself in a serious crisis, which was a consequence of economic difficulties, emergent nationalisms and in-fighting amongst the communist elite. The causes and driving forces of the Yugoslavian crisis have been explored elsewhere (Ramet 1999; Pavković 2000). However, the crisis led to new thinking about national identity among Slovenes, particularly in relation to the "southern brother nations" and to Western Europe. This thinking relied on assumptions about lazy, corrupt, dirty, Oriental foreigners, who were alleged to be leeching Slovenia's economy dry, whereas without them Slovenia could already have caught up with Western Europe (Žižek 1990: 55). Thus a period of intensive differentiation between Slovenes and other Yugoslavians began, a movement that has ideological, political and economic dimensions and which resulted in Slovenia's gaining of independence in 1991.

These "non-immigrant" burek eaters in the 1980s were primarily college students, punk rockers, and urban youths in general. At the level of meaning, as Stankovič adds, this means that the burek soon was not signifying only ethnic differences (between "Slovenes" and "non-Slovenes"), but also those Slovenes who did not have any major problems with the presence of immigrants from other republics of former Yugoslavia (Stankovič 2005: 36). However, according to conversations with the protagonists of urban subcultures (and urban vagabonds) in the 1980s, in those times the burek was not a sign or a symbolic object within various subcultural groups, nor was it a significant, important part of subcultural consumption. One prominent member of the generation of punk rockers from the late 1970s and early 80s (who were to play a significant role in Slovenia's liberalization and independence movement, see Lovšin, Mlakar & Vidmar 2002) says that food was not a part of subcultural expression among the punks – as opposed to punk cuisine in the USA, where it is a complex subcultural food system, with its own grammar, logic, and symbolism (Clark 2004). "Part of the subculture was drinking alcohol, mainly in the form of beer." One representative of the generation "which was politically and culturally socialized around the time of the first *Novi rok* (New Rock) concert (1981)", has this to say: "This whole thing with bureks in my opinion is more of a coincidence than anything else. Anyhow, at one in the morning the only thing open was a burek kiosk and nothing else. So once in a while I had a burek. […] I didn't usually do that. If some kiosk had been serving something else at one in the morning, I might have gone for polenta." And it was no different even outside of Ljubljana. One informant recalls the "punk times in the mining town of Idrija": "At least in the circle of people whom I hung out with at the time, I didn't have any kind of 'food-fetishism', of course as long as you don't count alcohol, which I wasn't too selective about, as food. The only important thing was price-performance." So the great majority of people who ate (or did not eat) bureks in the 1980s did not understand it as an explicitly political gesture. The burek was not (yet) politicized in the first half of the 80s. For urban youth, as well as everyone else who occasionally ate bureks, it was, as the conversations indicate, a source of calories, not symbols. However, this simplistic, plastic division is highly problematic. Semanticizing, according to Roland Barthes (1969: 12), is unavoidable: "as soon as there is a society, every usage is converted into a sign of itself". Thus, the purpose of a burek is to be filling, and that purpose cannot be separated from a sign for food. And I could go on and on. A burek is intended to be filling in a hurry, and this purpose cannot be separated from a sign for fast food. A burek is intended to be filling when everything else is closed, and this purpose cannot be separated from a sign for food for night-owls, etc.

At any rate, the burek made it possible to get something warm to put in an alcohol-laden stomach, something cheap for shallow pockets and something that was available even at the most impossible hours in the already very modest "socialist" range of products and services available in the 1980s. Again, in those times in the majority of the larger Slovenian towns, with a few exceptions (primarily hot dogs and chips), bureks were the only warm food available late at night and in the early morning (for more on consumption patterns in socialist Slovenia and Yugoslavia see Luthar 2010; for more on the "culture of everyday life" see Luthar & Pušnik 2010; for more on the disconnect between the social liberalization of the 80s and socialist consumption see Hyder Patterson 2011). And this is probably the crucial – though not the only significant – impetus in the burek's march onto this stage of signifying, discourses and nationalism.

The essential point of this early burek narrative of consuming "calories without symbols" is therefore that the "immigrant", "Balkan", "southern" burek found its way onto Slovenian streets, and worked its way to "non-immigrants", that is Slovenes. The fact of this "non-Slovene", "immigrant", "foreign" burek being in the hands and mouths of Slovenes bothered some people – those who, to use Stankovič's words, had problems "with the presence of immigrants from other republics of the former Yugoslavia". It is from this point on that the story of the burek and nationalism starts to become more complicated, to grow in increasingly interesting and complex ways. To make slightly free use of Thomas' (1991) syntagm, when the burek's presence bothers someone, it becomes a "socially entangled object". It is therefore very important to the burek's semantic genesis that the burek was a visible object, or better an object of observation – one of the rare (food) objects of observation on Slovenian streets at that time, when there were no kebabs, pizza by the slice, hamburgers etc., that is "western fare", in urban areas. The burek thus becomes an object of the nationalistic gaze, it is noticed and talked about in nationalist discourse, which treats it as a some kind of representative of anything "foreign", "Balkan", or "southern". Food, as was probably most convincingly demonstrated by Pierre Bourdieu (1984), structures our lives in a very complex manner, most often completely subconsciously. Furthermore, as Richard Wilk (1997: 183) argues, "distaste and rejection is often more important than taste and consumption in making social distinctions". And the burek in its early "semantic years" made a good case for this assertion – it was more significant in forming identities for those who did not consume it than for those who did (cf. Savaş 2014).

Thus the dominant meanings which defined the burek throughout the 1980s and 90s (and in the present day) were not produced in their primary, original forms by burek eaters. What was at work was (and still is) a nationalist discourse which did not accept the burek as its own, that is "ours". In other words, it was bothered by the presence and visibility of the burek on Slovenian streets, in the hands and mouths of youths and all others who occasionally ate bureks. The nationalist discourse thus focused its attention on the burek, and the burek was no longer just food, but also a signifier, a symbol, or a metaphor. It didn't fill Slovenes with just calories, but with symbols as well.

The graffito "Burek? Nein danke", which appeared in a street in the capital city of Ljubljana in the second half of the 1980s and has occasionally reappeared on the town's walls since then, is one of the earliest and most explicit nationalist "uses" of the burek.

Another probably less explicit but earlier nationalist reference – of which countless examples could be listed – is found in the 1986 song *Jasmina* by the group Agropop – one of Slovenia's most popular pop bands in the 80s. A female voice (Jasmina) sings the refrain in Serbo-Croatian over a distinctly Balkan melody, which speaks of the love of an immigrant and/or a Balkan person for the Slovenian Jasmina:

He was truly, a real man,
He smelled strongly of horse.
He has a really hairy back.
He got me with a cheese burek.

While it is possible to ask whether Agropop's song is at all politically or nationalistically motivated, there is no ambiguity in the case of a project called

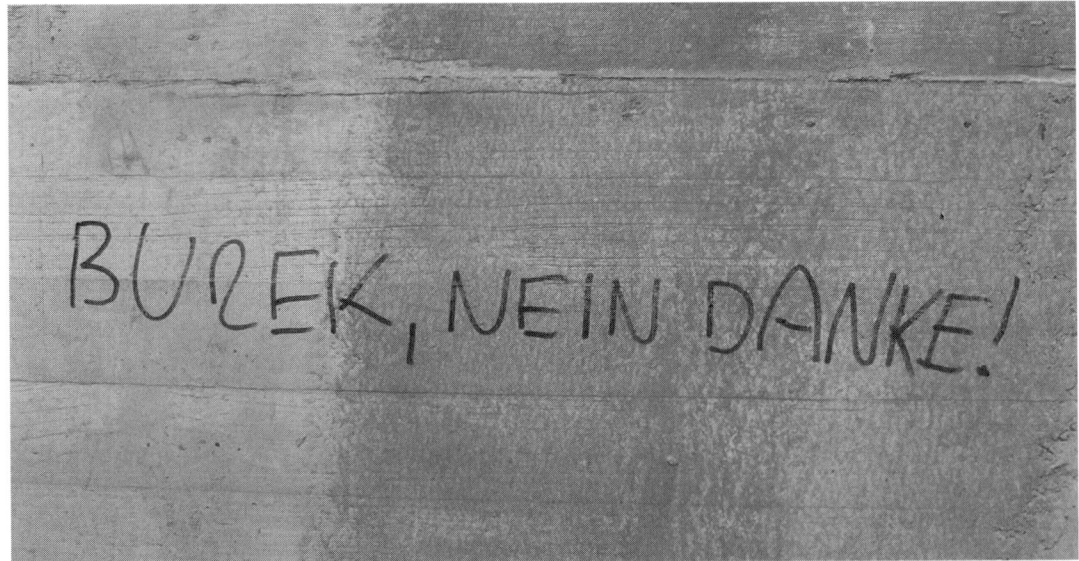

Ill. 2: Graffito in a Ljubljana street. Photo by the author.

"Anti Burek Sistem (A.B.S.)" by the skinhead group SLOI, which recited its texts in verse at pub counters. The project, by a group from the early 1990s, which played without instruments, is most likely a very explicit, highly motivated, dutiful nationalist burek statement. According to Arjun Appadurai (1981: 494), food is "a marvellously plastic kind of collective representation" with the "capacity of mobilizing strong emotions". Thus, a nationalist assault against the burek began in the second half of the 80s and flared up during breakup of Yugoslavia (for more on this see Mlekuž 2015). It is worth taking a moment to seek an understanding of how this assault functioned.

The process of self-definition, as was masterfully shown by Edward Said (1978[2003]), includes the dramatization of differences with others. It should be noted here that on the territory of present-day Slovenia, before the arrival of immigrants during the time of the SFRY, there was already a dish or several versions of a dish that was very similar to the burek in both form and manner of preparation. But it was not called a burek.[8] For the "Slovenian" burek therefore it is a case of the "narcissism of minor differences", as Freud (1905[1991]: 279) called it, where "minor differences in people who are otherwise alike [...] form the basis of feelings of strangeness and hostility between them". But it would probably be wrong to view and define the Slovenian "anti burek sistem" solely as an attack. As stated above, the burek is becoming increasingly more naturalized or incorporated into Slovenian society and culture. This incorporation or inclusion, according to Dick Hebdige (1979), proceeds on two levels, via two processes: (a) via the conversion of alternative or oppositional signs – that is signs which stand in opposition to the dominant culture – into mass-produced products, which Hebdige (1979) called the commodity form, and (b) via the labelling and redefining of practices, styles, behaviour, and things which are annoying to the dominant culture by dominant groups, so that they conform to and belong within their conceptual frameworks – what Hebdige called the ideological form. In this process of ideological and conceptual inclusion, these non-conformist practices and things which are annoying to the dominant culture can be (b1) on the one hand trivialized, naturalized, and domesticated – thus differentness is transformed into equality, and difference is denied, and (b2) on the other hand, as Hebdige (1979: 97) shows, this differentness can be turned into a spectacle, a clown show, or a scandal – thus difference is emphasized or manufactured. Probably the most bizarre product of this incorporation, which simultaneously offers varying interpretations (a clown show or denial of difference), the Carniolan burek – as read on the manufacturer's website – is "a Slovenian version of the most popular dish in the Balkans!" Carniola was the central Slovenian (and the most Slovenian) region of the Austro-Hungarian Empire, and the adjective continues to be used today to adorn numerous items considered to be Slovenian *par excellence*, including the flagship of Slovenian cuisine, the Carniolan sausage. The Carniolan burek was launched onto the market in 2013 by the industrial food processing company (and Slovenia's largest producer of baked goods) Žito, whose website states the following about their new product: "Slovenia's most popular quick snack has finally arrived with a traditional Slovenian taste" (Žito 2013). The "traditional Slovenian taste" of "Slovenia's most popular quick snack" is provided by pieces of Carniolan sausage and cabbage which are added to a cottage cheese filling. The Slovenian colonization of the (Carniolan) burek is further demarked by the Slovenian flag, which is stuck into this "Carniolan" or "Slovenian" product.[9]

However, the integration process of immigrant and foreign food in general can be highly varied and complex. For example, the doner kebab, which was brought to Germany by Turkish immigrants, played a central role in the recognition of that migrant group. At the places where Turks first sold doner kebabs as an exotic ethnic food (which was mainly bought by Germans) and was used as a positive symbol of cultural connection in multicultural discourse, the effects of the changing attitude towards foreigners led to a loosening of the association between "Turkishness" and the doner kebab. Stands and chains appeared with names like McKebap and Donerburger. At the same time, "doner" became a sobriquet for Turks. A multicultural youth festival in Berlin in 1987 was called "Disco doner", and the following slogan appeared in controversies about immigrants (*Ausländerfrage*): "Kein doner ohne Ausländer!" ("No immigrants, no kebabs!") Amidst this political chaos the doner kebab sold better than ever. But for Turks the continued association with it means a further denial of their increasing social mobility. The final irony is that in their attempts to loosen and move away from the association with the doner kebab, the sellers of this food moved into selling Italian food (Caglar 1995).

But let's go back to the beginning, to the cause of this nationalist interest in the burek. The appearance of the "Balkan", "Turkish", "southern" burek on Slovenian streets, and its increasing popularity and visibility, undoubtedly engendered nationalistic sentiments. But it is probably an exaggeration, if not actually wrong, to lay all of the blame for the parasitizing of the burek by nationalism on the appearance and visibility of the burek alone. There could also be other impetuses, though they are significantly less important, if they are important at all. As an example of such an external impetus, I might mention the silver medal won by Slovenian skier Jure Franko at the Olympics in Sarajevo in 1984 – Yugoslavia's first medal at a winter Olympics. The wordplay "Volimo Jureka više od bureka" ("We love Jurek more than burek", in Serbo-Croatian), which appeared at the time and is still remembered by many Slovenes, can still occasionally be found in humorous contexts in Slovenian media, pop culture and everyday speech, and undoubtedly brought the burek closer to Slovenes.[10] For example, in 2002 an article about a round-table discussion entitled "Slovenes and the Balkans: On the Europeanization of Slovenian society and the flight from the Balkans" in the newspaper *Več* carried the headline: "From Jure to the burek and other stories" (Stepišnik 2002: 5). And I could continue to list factors which brought the burek into the sphere of Slovenian nationalism. One of them, to continue in this vein, is probably that burek does not just rhyme with Jurek (a diminutive of the Slovenian name Jure), but also with Turek (Slovene for "Turk"). Turk, in the Slovenian (and to a great extent the European) popular imagination, (still) connotes a threatening Other (see Muršič 2010; Jezernik 2010). And this is even reflected in the titles and descriptions of burek recipes: "So that the burek will not be a Turek", or "a little more SLO[venian] and veggie, mushrooms for a change" (Šalehar 2004: 57).

The discussion of how the burek and nationalist discourse became intertwined also touches on Slovenia's independence in 1991. This event brought about the end of the official Yugoslav policy and ideology of brotherhood and unity. But nationalism clothed in popular discourse was already at work in the 1980s and earlier. The burek did not become a victim of nationalism because of Slovenia's independence, but independence – with all of its attendant changes and shocks to society and culture – undoubtedly draped the burek in much more diverse and colourful clothing.

Objects and Subjects

After Slovenia's independence, the burek decidedly becomes an *object* of alternative or oppositional praxis, which is easiest and most simply interpreted within the framework of the burek's important and visible semantic place in Slovenian culture and society – that is, as a response or even resistance to the (growing) nationalism (on nationalism in independent Slovenia see Pajnik 2002; Mlekuž 2008b). But this probably would not have happened to the burek if it had not had a special place within the available range of products and consumption at that time, and thus (again) it is also necessary to understand the socially conditioned rationalities (vis-à-vis the burek). Conversations with youths in the 1990s testify to how the burek very quickly became a popular and even revered part of the diet primarily among young urbanites, college and secondary-school students. Although it is difficult to shed sufficient light on the complex relationship between this "burek-loving" discourse and the consumption of bureks, it is not hard to identify the socio-cultural background to this relationship.

Peter Stankovič (1999: 46) says that a rebellious spirit began to spread primarily among urban youths who expressed ambivalence towards the project of Slovenia's independence. As an example of the initial manifestations of this rebellious spirit, Stankovič refers to a party which occurred completely spontaneously at the cult club B-51 in Ljubljana on the exact day of the declaration of Slovenian independence, June 25, 1991: "At the moment when all of Slovenia was celebrating its secession from Yugoslavia, a crowd of young people danced and drank beer until morning to the nostalgic sounds of Yugo rock, and at the end they were partying to the wild rhythms of Serbian turbo folk"[11] (Stankovič 1999: 46). This rebellious spirit manifested itself in a love of all things "Balkan" and "southern". This was not in fact a political movement, Stankovič continues, but brought about or constituted an interesting cultural reversal, in which for part of the urban youth (primarily college students, alternative types, secondary-school students etc.), everything Balkan changed from a symbol for the bad into a symbol of the good. Thus it was a deviation which stood in opposition to the "official", dominant nationalistic discourse:

> In an instant, so-called Balkan parties were everywhere, pop and rock music from the former Yugoslavia became "the law", even for those who were too young to have grown up with their sounds, the use of Serbo-Croatian in vernacular speech increased to truly unbelievable proportions, bureks and baklava became the height of fashion, famous Serbian comedy films (Who's Singin' over there, The Marathon Family, Balkan Spy, The Fall of Rock and Roll etc.) became references to be cited as often as possible, in short, a certain nostalgic sentiment spread among the urban youth which probably more than anything else reflected a certain fear that life in independent Slovenia would become too "Austrian": closed, cold-hearted, buttoned-down and provincial. (Stankovič 1999: 46)

Or as one of my informants historically analysed his love: "[...] at the beginning of the 80s, when nobody even dreamed that the country would break apart, I also couldn't have Yugonostalgia, which was probably responsible for my later love of bureks". Thus, the love of the liberated youth and other love for the burek is associated with a certain nostalgia, which at least in certain segments and cases can also be understood as a sort of implicit rebellion against the dominant popular and also the multitude of official nationalist discourses in the newly formed country (for more on anti-nationalism in the Yugoslav context, see Bilić & Janković 2012). So the burek is consistently encoded as non-Slovenian, by nationalists and rebels alike.

According to Stankovič (2005: 36), primarily among the younger urban population, among college and secondary-school students, the burek began to function increasingly as a sign for something cool, and also began to affix other meanings to the concepts of the South and the Balkan. These alternative political meanings, which were more or less in diametrical opposition to the nationalist discourse, were probably more of an alternative than an oppositional discourse (the line between them, as Raymond Williams pointed out, often being blurry).[12]

One of the first articulations of this alternative discourse was the bureks that were handed out at the entrances or used as entry tickets to various "Balkan parties" in various clubs in Ljubljana at the beginning of the 1990s. At the first Balkan party, on May 24, 1991 at the B-51 club, upon purchasing their tickets at the entrance, guests received a shot of rakia and a burek, filled with Serbian cheese, onions and bread. But in fact, the most frequent articulation or statement of this alternative discourse was simply eating a burek. As conversations with college students in the 90s (as well as my own memories) testify, the merrymaking at so-called Balkan parties and other student parties at which Yugo music was an important element, often ended with a burek. Eating bureks was a kind of ritual conclusion to a night of partying.

"Burek eating" was also often accompanied by other "burek-loving" activities. Consumption, particularly the consumption of such meaning-laden things as the burek, is not a solitary, unique phenomenon, but is embedded in a network of other associations and activities. The burek is thus frequently found in youth and student magazines, groups, songs etc. For instance, in the name of the first anthology of an original comic from Eastern Europe, Stripburek, in the name of the acting troupe Burekteater, in the song "Burek, oj, oj, oj" by the garage rock band Kripelbataljon – to give just three more or less random examples from this unmanageably long list. In short, the burek becomes a very popular object, used frequently and in various ways, and often even an object of veneration among urban youth, which further provokes and motivates nationalists to aim their arrows at it more often. So the burek helps to create a special and distinctive national/transnational sense of belonging (that does not exclude the shared experience of the former Yugoslavia) in what Appadurai (1996) has called new "ethnoscapes".

However, at least from the mid-90s on, the background to this anti-nationalistic discourse cannot in any way be reduced to nostalgic commemoration of the former SFRY and/or worshipping of the South, the Balkan, brotherhood and unity. If I said that the initial, original meanings of the burek among the young urban population, among college and secondary-school students, were more or less diametrically opposed to the nationalist discourse, but that they could probably only rarely be labelled as an explicit rebellion against nationalism – that is, it was more likely an alternative rather than an oppositional discourse – from the mid-90s on there were increasing numbers of explicit, politically engaged statements which touched on the burek in one way or another. And if I said that this alternative, implicit discourse at least to a certain extent coincides with a type of "burek-loving" discourse which is to a great extent formed and represented by burek-eaters, it rarely if ever appears or is reflected in utterances, in contrast to the explicit, oppositional practice of eating bureks. Thus in this explicit, oppositional discourse, the burek is not an object of veneration in and of itself, but is merely a signifier. This signifier occupies a subordinate position in the existing power relations, which indicates a lack of strength. Of course, such a division can be problematic, as the line between the explicit and the implicit, between oppositional and alternative, as noted above, is often blurred or erased. One example of an explicit, oppositional discourse is the aforementioned graffito "I'll have a burek, but not a mosque", which touches on the long and heated debate over the (non-)construction of a mosque in the Slovenian capital (Ljubljana is probably one of the few European capitals that still does not have a mosque), or the title of the article "Burek? Ja, Bitte" (Stankovič 2005), a paraphrase of another aforementioned graffito, in which the response to the burek is primarily a defence of immigrants and their culture: "[T]he burek [can] also be seen completely differently as a symbol. Not as a symbol of backwardness and a lack of civility, i.e. 'the Balkans', but exactly the opposite, as a symbol of the contribution of the culture of immigrants from former Yugoslav republics to the civilizing of Slovenia itself" (Stankovič 2005: 36). The burek thus becomes or is a distinctive, powerful "intertextual" object in the sense that the meanings that are imputed to it are in-

Ill. 3: The cover of "Stripburek: Comics from behind the Rusty Iron Curtain", a special edition of the comic Stripburger. Courtesy of Stripburger, Forum Ljubljana.

fluenced by printed, broadcast and other statements (cf. Hebdige 1979: 80–84).

Let's return to the youth and their adoption and consumption of the burek, to the material level of production of meaning, where it is necessary to understand – and this needs to be emphasised – the place of the burek among the fast foods available at that time and in particular the food that was available at the most "impossible" hours. I believe that it is taking a very narrow view to see the burek merely as a symbolic object which students and other youth in the 1990s chose *solely* due to its symbolic weight, its symbolic position – that is because of its semantic associations with immigrants, the Balkans, the SFRY and related phenomena. One first has to ask what was even available at that time at an affordable price, anytime, anywhere, and with at least a minimal possibility of choice (i.e. cheese, meat or apple). Students and other youths in the 90s did not eat bureks primarily because they were "Balkan" or "southern", or because it represented a rebellion against the dominant nationalist discourse. They did so mainly because they were cheap, filling, very accessible at least in urban areas, and because, as several of informants stated, "it sat perfectly in an alcohol-laden belly". If it was primarily about symbols, then the students would have chosen *čevapčiči*, which at least through the 1980s were a more symbolically laden food than the burek – and they were frequently called upon when people were looking for a signifier of the South, the Balkans, and southerners. For example, in the provocative, nationalistically galvanizing and highly influential article by Slovenian critic, essayist and editor Bojan Štih entitled "That's Not a Poem, That's Just Love", published in Slovenia's leading cultural magazine *Naši razgledi* (Our Views) in 1982, as well as the fiery polemics which that article provoked in nearly all of the major Yugoslav print media of the time, there is no mention of the burek – but we do find *čevapčiči* (Mlekuž 2015).

However, this "banal", pragmatic, material fact does not invalidate the role played by the burek among youths. To put it more ambitiously, the practices associated with the burek and its transformation significantly informed youth culture in the 90s (cf. Hebdige 1979). The burek externalized meanings and values, made them visible and intelligible for further actions by subjects. The burek "provides the basis on which subjects [youths] come into being, rather than simply answering their pre-existing needs" (Myers 2001: 21). Or in Miller's words: the burek "represents culture, not because [it is] merely there as environment within which we operate, but because [it is] an integral part of the process of objectification by which we create ourselves as an industrial society: our identities, our social affiliations, our lived everyday practices" (Miller 1987: 215). The burek was the very medium through which the youth made and knew themselves. It did not simply reflect pre-existing meanings and social distinctions but actively participated in the reproduction and transformation of these meanings and social distinctions. It did far more than just express meaning. Bureks and youths – objects and subjects – are inseparably connected in a dialectical relationship of creating each other.

Conclusion

On the level of meanings, two more or less opposite positions can be identified with respect to the burek, with very little common dialogue. The burek in immigrant families is a part of a residual unincorporated culture which is significantly removed from the dominant culture. The fast food burek from Slovenian streets is, on the other hand, part of the incorporated emergent culture and subject to various discourses, particularly the nationalistic one. It is probably the handiest and most frequently used signifier in Slovenian popular culture, media, vernacular language etc. for immigrants from the former republics of the SFRY, the Balkans, the SFRY and the phenomena associated with it.

The crucial importance to the burek's semantic inflation was the simple and banal fact that in the 1980s the burek was one of the rare products available late at night, that it was warm and cheap and that it was probably one of the very few visible dietary objects – objects of observation – on Slovenian streets. The burek's presence bothered some people, it became an object of the nationalistic gaze, it was noticed and talked about in nationalist discourse, which treated it as a some kind of representative of anything "foreign", "immigrant", "Balkan". In this case, the burek was more significant in forming identities for those who did not consume it than for those who did. So, the burek attracted meanings, and made them visible and intelligible so that they could be further employed by subjects. Its meanings turned out to be significant.

After Slovenia gained its independence in 1991, the burek became a popular and even revered part of the diet primarily among young urbanites, college and secondary-school students, an object of alternative or oppositional praxis associated with a positive attitude towards immigrants, the Balkans, the SFRY and related phenomena, and even an object of adoration and worship. But students and other youths in the 90s did not eat bureks primarily because they were Balkan or southern, or because it represented a rebellion against the dominant nationalist discourse. They did so mainly because they were cheap, filling, very accessible at least in urban areas, and because they "sat perfectly in an alcohol-laden belly". However, this "banal", material fact does not reduce the role that bureks played among young people. Bureks actively participated in the process through which the youth made and knew themselves. Its appropriation enabled a highly creative and productive process of (re)production of subjectivities, identities, and groups. The burek does not just reflect or represent meaning, but intervenes, makes a difference, and alters people's minds.

Notes

1 From February 20, 2008, to January 24, 2017, it had 353,167 views, which is undoubtedly a huge success on the Slovene market of just over two million people.
2 Bureks were served at the Sultan's table at least as far back as the 15th century, and a recipe for burek first appears in a Turkish legal text (*kanun*) in 1501/02 (Zirojević 2014).
3 In the original: We asked for workers. We got people instead.
4 Despite its relative distance from the dominant culture, a residual culture can be incorporated into it through concrete activities. "By 'emergent' I mean, first, that new meanings and values, new practices, new significances and experiences, are continually being created. But there is a much earlier attempt to incorporate them, just because they are part – and yet not a defined part – of effective contemporary practice" (Williams 2005: 41).
5 In a telephone survey by the daily newspaper *Delo* it took second place (14.3%) behind the winner, "pizza by the slice" (27.1%) and ahead of hamburgers (11.1%), sandwiches (8.6%), French fries (7.1%), hot dogs (4.4%) and kebabs (4.2%). In urban environments there are significantly more burek, hamburger and kebab fans, while in rural areas pizza and French fries enjoy above-average popularity. The proportion of burek lovers also increases with the level of education of the respondents. Among people with higher education the burek even trumps pizza and takes first place at 23.3%, with pizza in second place at one percent lower. The telephone survey asked: "Which of the following is your favourite type of fast food?" They also asked what kind of burek was the respondents' favourite. The most popular was the cheese burek (47.3%), followed by meat (16.7%), apple (10.6%) and pizza burek (4.7%). The telephone survey was conducted on February 25, 2005, on a sample of 406 people (Pal 2005: 13).
6 See https://www.kulinarika.net/iskanje/?splosno_besede=klobasa+&imageField.x=0&imageField.y=0.
7 Nationalism was also present before the 1980s in the form of popular and other discourses. For instance Gorazd Stariha (2006), through an analysis of documents kept in the archives of the Petty Offences Magistrate in Radovljica and the Radovljica District Court, demonstrated that as early as the 1950s in upper Gorenjska there were several cases of expressions of intolerance, chicanery, and even physical violence directed at immigrants from other republics of the SFRY.
8 Various types of flatbreads and cakes made of phyllo dough which were similar to the burek in appearance, preparation and content were known primarily in the south-western and south-eastern parts of Slovenia (e.g. *prleška oljovica, presni kolač, pršjača, belokranjska povitica, prosta povitica*). These were prepared primarily as holiday and ritual dishes and dishes prepared at the end of major agricultural jobs. However, technical and other similarities still do not constitute an argument for one or another kind of influence or even a common origin of the dishes.
9 The Carniolan burek is an example of a so-called hybrid dish – dishes created on the basis of cultural mixing and creolization, and which in the long historical perspective are probably the rule rather than the exception (cf. Delamont 1995). The question that arises (and which was posed to me in numerous interviews and conversations) is whether the burek can become a "Slovenian dish", that is a Slovenian dietary icon. The

answer is affirmative, as the biographies or histories of numerous dishes bear witness to the fact that such conceptual changes or transitions can occur in a relatively short period of time. For instance, up to the 1970s the donut, today a Canadian icon, was presented in the Canadian media as American food (and was in fact imported from the United States). In the 70s several restaurants began to advertise donuts, mainly in order to attract American tourists, and by the 80s it had appeared as a powerful symbol of Canadian life (Penfold 2008).

10 The graffito "Burek, nein danke" would probably never have appeared at all if not for the famous European anti-nuclear slogan from the early 1980s, "Atom, nein danke".

11 Turbo-folk is a musical genre – a mixture of Serbian folk music with modern pop music elements. Having mainstream popularity in Serbia, and although closely associated with Serbian performers, the genre is widely popular in Croatia, Slovenia, Bosnia and Herzegovina, Macedonia, Bulgaria and Montenegro.

12 The difference between the alternative and the oppositional is a difference, to use Williams' words, "between someone who simply finds a different way to live and wishes to be left alone with it, and someone who finds a different way to live and wants to change society in its light" (Williams 2005: 41–42). So the alternative reflects political passivity, while the oppositional is about political engagement in practices which represent a form of competition against or deviation from the dominant forms.

References

Appadurai, Arjun 1981: Gastro-Politics in Hindu South Asia. *American Ethnologist* 8, 494–511.

Appadurai, Arjun 1986: Introduction. In: Arjun Appadurai (ed.), *The Social Life of Things*: Commodities in Cultural Perspective. Cambridge & New York: Cambridge University Press, pp. 3–63.

Appadurai, Arjun 1996: *Modernity at Large: Cultural Dimensions of Globalization*. Minneapolis: University of Minnesota Press.

Barthes, Roland 1969: *Elements of Semiology*. London: Cape.

Bikić, Jasna 2004: Ja sam živi dokaz protiv riječi nemoguće. *Ljiljan*, June 11, p. 10.

Bilić, Bojan & Vesna Janković (eds.) 2012: *Resisting the Evil: [Post]-Yugoslav Anti-War Contention*. Baden-Baden: Nomos.

Bourdieu, Pierre 1984: *Distinction: A Social Critique of the Judgement of Taste*. London & New York: Routledge.

Caglar, Ayse 1995: McDoner: Doner Kebap and the Social Positioning Struggle of German Turks. In: Janeen Arnold Costa & Gary J. Bamossy (eds.), *Marketing in a Multicultural World: Ethnicity, Nationalism, and Cultural Identity*, pp. 209–230.

Clark, Dylan 2004: The Raw and the Rotten: Punk Cuisine. *Ethnology* 43:1, 19–31.

Delamont, Sarah 1995: *Appetites and Identities: An Introduction to the Social Anthropology of Western Europe*. London: Routledge.

Freud, Sigmund 1905[1991]: *On Sexuality: Three Essays on the Theory of Sexuality and other Works*. London: Penguin.

Gell, Alfred 1998: *Art and Agency: An Anthropological Theory*. Oxford: Clarendon.

Gregory, A. Christopher 1982: *Gift and Commodities*. London: Academic Press.

Hebdige, Dick 1979: *Subculture: The Meaning of Style*. London & New York: Methuen & Co.

Hebdige, Dick 1988: *Hiding in the Light: On Images and Things*. London: Routledge.

Hyder Patterson, Patrick 2001: *Bought and Sold: Living and Losing the Good Life in Socialist Yugoslavia*. Ithaca & London: Cornell University Press.

Jezernik, Božidar 2010: Imagining 'the Turk'. In: Božidar Jezernik (ed.), *Imagining 'the Turk'*. Newcastle upon Tyne: Cambridge Scholars, pp. 1–16.

Josipovič, Damir 2006: Pregled strukture selitvenih tokov iz BiH v okviru notranje-jugoslovanskih migracij v Slovenijo. *Annales: Series historia et sociologia* 16:2, 285–306.

Josipovič, Damir 2012: Social Solidarity in Post-Socialist Countries. In: Marion Ellison (ed.), *Reinventing Social Solidarity across Europe*. Bristol: Policy Press, pp. 157–190.

Lovšin, Peter, Peter Mlakar & Igor Vidmar (eds.) 2002: *Punk je bil prej: 25 let punka pod Slovenci*. Ljubljana: Cankarjeva založba.

Luthar, Breda 2010: Shame, Desire and Longing for the West: A Case Study of Consumption. In: Breda Luthar & Maruša Pušnik (eds.), *Remembering Utopia: The Culture of Everyday Life in Socialist Yugoslavia*. Washington DC: New Academic Publishing, pp. 341–378.

Luthar, Breda & Maruša Pušnik (eds.) 2010: *Remembering Utopia: The Culture of Everyday Life in Socialist Yugoslavia*. Washington DC: New Academic Publishing.

Mauss, Marcel 1954: *The Gift: The Forms and Functions of Exchange in Archaic Societies*. London: Cohen and West Ltd.

Miller, Daniel 1987: *Material Culture and Mass Consumption*. Oxford & New York: Blackwell.

Miller, Daniel 1994: Artefacts and the Meaning of Things. In: Tim Ingold (ed.), *Companion Encyclopedia of Anthropology*. London & New York: Routledge, pp. 396–419.

Miller, Daniel 1998: Why Some Things Matter. In: Daniel Miller (ed.), *Material Cultures: Why Some Things Matter*. London: UCL Press, pp. 3–21.

Miller, Daniel 2010: *Stuff*. Cambridge: Polity Press.

Mlekuž, Jernej 2008a: *Burek.si?! Koncepti/Recepti*. Ljubljana: Studia humanitatis.

Mlekuž, Jernej 2008b: Čapac.si, or on Burekalism and its Bites: An Analysis of Selected Images of Immigrants and their Descendants in Slovenian Media and Popular Culture. *Dve domovini / Two Homelands* 28, 23–37.

Mlekuž, Jernej 2017: When the Grease Runs through the Paper: On the Consumption of Ultragreasy Bureks. In: Jürgen Martschukat & Bryant Simon (eds.), *Food, Power and Agency*. London & New York: Bloomsbury Academic, pp. 169–190.

Muršič, Rajko 2010: On Symbolic Othering: 'The Turk' as a Threatening Other. In: Božidar Jezernik (ed.), *Imagining 'the Turk'*. Newcastle upon Tyne: Cambridge Scholars, pp. 17–26.

Myers, R. Fred 2001: Introduction: Commodities and the Politics of Value In: Fred R. Myers (ed.), *The Empire of Things: Regimes of Value and Material Culture*. Santa Fe: School of American Research Press, pp. 4–64.

Pajnik, Mojca 2002: *Xenophobia and Post-Socialism*. Ljubljana: Peace Institute.

Pal, Nejc 2005: Mesni ali sirni? Sirni. *Več*, March 4, p. 13.

Pavković, Aleksandar 2000: *The Fragmentation of Yugoslavia: Nationalism and War in the Balkans*. London: Macmillan.

Penfold, Steve 2008: *The Donut: A Canadian History*. Toronto: University of Toronto Press.

Ramet, Sabrina 1999: *Balkan Babel: The Disintegration of Yugoslavia from the Death of Tito to the Insurrection in Kosovo*. Boulder, CO: Westview Press.

Razvezani jezik 2012: Burek. Available at: http://razvezanijezik.org/?page=burek (accessed June 19, 2014).

Said, Edward W. 1978[2003]: *Orientalism*. London: Penguin.

Šalehar, Matevž 2004: Da burek ne bo Turek. *Več*, January 23, p. 57.

Savaş, Özlem 2014: Taste Diaspora: The Aesthetic and Material Practice of Belonging. *Journal of Material Culture* 19:2, 185–208.

Stankovič, Peter 1999: Rokerji s konca tisočletja. In: Peter Stankovič, Tomc Gregor & Velikonja Mitja (eds.), *Urbana plemena: Subkulture v Sloveniji v devetdesetih*. Ljubljana: Študentska založba, pp. 43–52.

Stankovič, Peter 2005: Burek? Ja, bitte! *Dnevnik, Zelena pika*, January 15, p. 7.

Stariha, Gorazd 2006: Dvigam to čašo za bratstvo in enotnost naših narodov. *Zgodovina za vse* 13:2, 83–114.

Stepišnik, Matija 2002: Od Jureta do bureka in druge zgodbe. *Več*, November 25, p. 5.

Thomas, Nicholas 1991: *Entangled Objects: Exchange, Material Culture, and Colonialism in the Pacific*. Cambridge: Harvard University Press.

Trio Genialci 2008: Ti si burek. Available at: http://www.youtube.com/results?search_query=ti+si+burek (accessed January 24, 2017).

Wilk, Richard 1997: A Critique of Desire: Distaste and Dislike in Consumer Behaviour. *Consumption, Markets and Culture* 1:2, 2.

Williams, Raymond 2005: *Culture and Materialism: Selected Essays*. London: Verso.

Zirojević, Olga 2014: Burek. Available at: http://www.mediantrop.rankomunitic.org/olga-zirojevic-burek?fb_action_ids=10152453028704274&fb_action_types=og.likes (accessed June 11, 2014).

Žito 2013: Kranjski burek. Available at: http://kruh.zito.si/2013/05/kranjski/ (accessed June 19, 2014).

Žižek, Slavoj 1990: Eastern Europe's Republics of Gilead. *New Left Review* 183, 50–62.

Jernej Mlekuž is a research fellow at the Slovenian Migration Institute at the Research Centre of the Slovenian Academy of Sciences and Arts. His research interests are migration theory and methodology, cultural aspects of migration processes, popular culture, media, nationalism, food studies, material culture, epistemology, and epiphenomena. Currently, he is finishing research on the sausage *kranjska klobasa*. He is the author of the prize-winning book *Burek: A Culinary Metaphor* (also published in Slovenian, Serbian and Albanian).
(Mlekuz@zrc-sazu.si)

SIEF membership package

In December 2014 the membership of SIEF, the Société Internationale d'Ethnologie et de Folklore, voted in favour of making *Ethnologia Europaea* its official journal, after SIEF, the editors and the publisher of *Ethnologia Europaea,* Museum Tusculanum Press, had prepared the ground for a mutually agreeable association between organization and publication. SIEF was founded in 1964, *Ethnologia Europaea* in 1966, and as recent historiographic research makes quite evident, there was no love lost between the actors founding the two respective institutions. Some five decades later, it is safe to say that cooperation rather than particularization is the major coin of scholarship. Both partners share a profound interest in nurturing and promoting scientific research and communication within our field(s), in extending international collaboration among European ethnologists as well as in disseminating new ethnological knowledge to a wide readership.

Membership

SIEF gathers every two years for its international congress, where colleagues engage with one another's work and enjoy each other's company. The SIEF congress is an intellectual festival that showcases the state of the art in our fields and a ritual time in the academic calendar, crucial for building professional networks, a number of collaborative projects, finding inspiration, and cultivating friendships. Between congresses, SIEF's numerous working groups provide platforms for critical debate, networking, and exchange of information; they organize their own meetings and sponsor publications.

SIEF has two professional journals: *Ethnologia Europaea*, a printed subscription-based journal that all members receive by mail twice a year, and *Cultural Analysis*, an Open Access journal published online. In addition, SIEF communicates with members through its website and with two newsletters sent out every year.

The annual membership fee is € 35. Opting for a two-year membership in one go qualifies for a discounted price of € 67. Membership will support SIEF to grow as a strong professional organization, while allowing members to participate in the SIEF community and shape the future of the academic fields.

The membership package offers a great host of benefits, including a subscription to the lively and interdisciplinary, peer-reviewed journal *Ethnologia Europaea*. Members will receive printed copies of the biannual journal as well as electronic access to available backlist issues.

See more and apply for membership now at www.siefhome.org.